CRAZY RICH HAWAII

Dr. Mia Morgan White

Los Angeles California

Printed in the United States of America

Library of Congress Control Number 2021940510

First Printing, 2021

ISBN: 978-1-60361-913-4
ISBN-13: 978-1-60361-913-4

My dedication to
Shakespeare, Freud, and Nietzsche.

Because men were being tortured all around the World.

CRAZY

RICH HAWAII

By DR MIA MORGAN WHITE

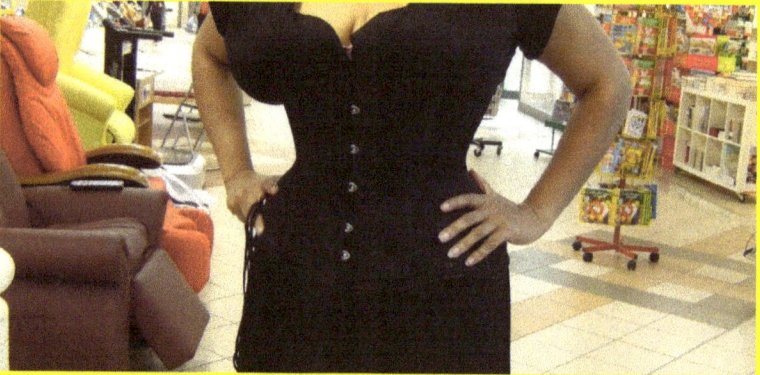

Introduction

Sometimes people think crimes of energy can't be seen. I am a witness. Walking through London, Hawaii, Cannes, Cairo, San Francisco, Los Angeles, Paris, Monaco, Venice and Brighton for Events.

My beloved Hawaii - and I as SNOW WHITE: WOMEN WHO ARE JEALOUS WILL TRY TO DESTROY YOUR LIFE

AMUSEMENT

Not Your Burger

My WORK HAS SAVED LIVES FOR 20 YEARS

ALICE: BE RARE IN ANY WORLD ESPECIALLY IN RABBIT HOLES

I specialize in the Brain

FULL BRAIN CAPACITY ENERGETIC WAVE PATTERNS and I am a the subconscious, cleaning, healing and reprogramming it. Cinderella

Lavender Fields

ARIEL loved the prince. FOR MY NEXT TRICK

CONSTRUCTED HOSTILE ENVIRONMENT

People Are Dying From Lack of Hope via an orchestrated manipulation.

THOUGHTS CAN SHAPE THE ENERGY

PANTHEONS COMPARE CROSS REFERENCE CHART

SCIENCE & MAGIC the ALCHEMY OF WHAT LOVE IS

KOI: KING OF INDUSTRY

SPEAK TO WATER

19 TREATING DNA SIGNAL STRENGTH VENICE

WINTER GOD PROVIDES

CINDERELLA WOMEN WHO CAN'T COMPARE WILL BLOCK YOUR MONEY

BEAUTY AND HER BEAST W/O FEAR nor was she given potions by TEMPTATION TO BE FAKE BY ENTICEMENT OF VERY HANDSOME MEN

FALL CLEANS DEBRIS OF ALL SEASONS AND DRIVES THE SEEDS INTO THE GROUND to build our new life.

Betrayals

Every moment is the present. Literally and figuratively.

Dr. Mia Morgan White

SUMMER BRINGS THE LIGHT NEEDED WE'LL CALL THIS CHAPTER *A Bat Out Of Hell*

A Bat Out Of Hell (You thought you liked dirty girls...)

The first time Richard told me in his plans to leave Hawaii and for us to live together, we had to put it on hold because Pele erupted and he lost hundreds of acres of land and he was disappointed and he said, He'd have to find another way because he'd been stuck there unhappy for 17 years. So, he needed time. He wanted me to close my business and give up my loft and be ready. Richard loved me so much. We'd known each other three months but he said he'd hoped his whole life a woman like me existed . He would call me the girl version of him.

The last time... well I'd like to say this, Jason, your father loved you very much. We came up with a plan when you tried to commit suicide that although he was leaving that week and had told his ex-wife.

And then your suicide happened. And so, we came up with a plan that we would wait until he could get you stable. Also, that we would use my energy, my light, every time they attacked to keep him there. And every time they attacked you to make you sad enough to want to commit suicide. So, we used my light to fill him and you to get you through that. He told me he was flying to China to take you so that you could be watched around the clock until he was okay. And it would be about six months to a year. So, we waited again.

So it's better to start back at the first time, Back to the first time Richard said give up everything and be with him, had not told me about anybody, not that he had kids or ex-wives or anything like that, he would just tell me about how he grew up in his childhood and young adulthood. He always wished a girl who looked like me would like his personality. And Like him back. And How he had in middle school and high school come up with a little illegal business and he would lie to his mother and say that his grandmother sent him money. But what he'd really done was he was buying marijuana. And then breaking it down into little small rolled cigs. I think it's joint cigarettes and selling them as a kid at school to other kids to make a profit. He grew up in a very violent place and wanted to protect his mother. And one time his mother found the money and wanted to know how he had come up with so much money.

And because she wanted to know the truth, Richard said, he told her that his grandmother had sent it to him, lying. So, when he flew me to Hawaii to prove that he was still trying, because we living together had been delayed 4 times by the time he flew me to Hawaii. That upon landing he showed me his grandmother's house and said that the family had just previously sold it. And you his son passed us on the road. I don't know if you knew that, but we didn't know to stop you or not. But he thought it was a good sign that, Hey, we saw you in a car passing us.

So, I had no idea. More than a year before, Richard just came out of the blue after, right out of the gate serious. You know, a lot of conversations, a lot of talking, a lot of texts, a lot of just talking about how miserable and unhappy he was and stuck there and that he was going to do everything he could to get himself out of there and leave.

Once he'd gotten to the monetary success and the ability to "get any woman he wanted" there were no girls like me where he'd come from who would fulfill his teen dreams. and let's admit it God had pulled me out of time: my aging, the type of woman I am, years passed since the last time I wanted to go to Hawaii, the clock stopped years ago when I moved to Europe.

So, he asked me quickly, the first time he asked was Pele's eruption soon after we met. And the last time was when he flew to California after your suicide to see me, he brought you with him. You were in the room next door, down the hall from us. And you text him about going to dinner at Denny's. While we were talking and coming up with a plan to keep you energetically safe from the attacks that were happening from the women he had been involved with sending energy attacks for years. And each time it would be something different, his health, his money and ruthless and attacks he had suffered years before he met me and attacks on me now. I didn't know that he had ex-wives. So in my line of work, Chinese Medicine and Energy is everywhere. I didn't know where it might be coming from because it was coming from envy. It = negative energy. There was some hate and some racism attached to all energy that was coming in and hitting things, but it was accredited to the wrong people until the fourth time Richard tried to leave, so we could go and live our lives together.

And that was when he told me that he had children and he actually didn't say I have children. He said, do you like children? And I remember saying, you know, I like kids they're okay. And he looked so disappointed. And then I said, you do realize that I taught school for decades and have four different credentials to teach. I love kids at every age. Why are you asking if I like kids? And he said, well, I have kids and I didn't want to tell you. Cause I thought you would leave me or actually first he said, I thought wouldn't like me and I didn't want you to leave. And I was like, why would I do that? And he said, well, I've got kids. And I said, okay, well I like them. and I love them if they are yours. And then he said, do you like dogs? Now, this was long before I met Moose but I call him Moosie Moosie. So, before I met his little furry self, he was Richards road dog. I used to hear him barking rarely when Richard would leave so distraught, so upset, so disappointed at the betrayal, the hate and the coldness that he was living with, that he would call me between , 10PM and 2:30 in the morning sometimes. he never called me flirting at that time of night.

Now every other time of day that he called there was only planning and flirting. All he did at those hard night times in Hawaii was blast 70s music. When I get up in the morning, I get up at five every morning for prayer and meditation. So, he would call me any time after 5:00 AM, California time, Pacific time and then wherever he was in the world he called me, he called me from Shanghai. He would call me and then he would flirt and joke and say like little stuff and code names that we had. And he, if he called me after 10 PM, I knew he was sad and upset, broken hearted and couldn't sleep in his own home. Because it was so cold and awful.

And so, he'd call me and he and moose would be in the car with the windows down and they would be blaring airing, 1970s, soul music. And he said, it's the only way I can have my youth. And I can have myself is when I'm in this car. Go to McDonald's with moose and driving, but now life is different "I get to call you". So, he had done this behavior for some time I think it was 10 years or more. I know he said he'd been unhappy for 17 years and to cheer him up I would tease him for eating McDonald's and he reminded me of the city where he grew up and I didn't grow up in a city like that. So, I could see it was comfort food, terrible for his body but the memories helped his soul, my students grew up in neighborhoods like that, so I knew the hardship and then he tells me Well, it's okay. I'm almost here now. I'm going to eat and then I'll call you at a reasonable hour. And I say, okay and then I talked to him in a few days or a couple of weeks, and each time he had some more progress that he had made on leaving Hawaii and selling 4140. But then. He said that every time he put the house on sale, something would happen to stop the sale and it would go off the market and then he would put it back on the market.

And each time he told the exes that he had been involved with, the wives and the girlfriends. That he was doing it. And then he'd be sad and say, I'm selling my family home, but I can't think of another way. And I said, why? And then he'd say, well, they're trying to take my company. If I leave it, I don't want to leave with nothing. So, I have to stay longer and find another plan.

So, I would like to say to Jason, please don't ever try to commit suicide again, because we gave up a lot to protect you because we both valued your life so much.

The Empress Embodies All Queens

So, the third time was it out? Eight months when you say it wasn't quite a year later that he was determined he was leaving and then he got a tapeworm and he got a lot of energy attacks, black magic. And so, did I. And so, there was no discussion of waiting. He said I had to sell my truck. And we would be on the road, he was going to buy some super fancy, $250,000.00 RV , I, he tried to talk me into it about this road vehicle and I after that call I was supposed to figure out the places I'd be willing to go and be because he said he needed some time where no one just come to an address he said we'd be on the road about a year. until he decided where would be best for us, to have our house.

So no one Could pinpoint him when they wanted to that he could just be free and we'd just be gone. And so, I was like, I love my truck and I don't want to sell it, but I have closed my business and I have given up my loft and I will drive my truck to all the types of places, That takes the kind of motor vehicle you're talking about and I'll scope out the places we could travel, camp in cities That would support my painting and meditation.

some fancy type he had rented and traveled in on a family vacation years before.

And he said, okay. And then he did his part and he called me on his birthday he called and he was so sad and said that, you know, nobody there really cared that he was alive. They just wanted money or they didn't understand what he was going through. And I realized towards the end of the phone call, it was the date of his birthday. I hadn't been taking coaching clients he'd told me no commitments to my work or homes so I could be ready like I promised he'd say to be ready. I don't map out days the way most people do I'm a very spiritual person and very scientific person at the same time. Richard called me 99. And I guess since he's dead, we don't, I don't have to keep our little secret code names so that in our texts and emails, we would know it was one another, he never presented it as we were keeping us hidden from anyone. He said he wasn't the only one who had access to his company email.

He just would say, He wanted me to know when it was him sending a message. And so. I'm a member of Mensa. That's, a genius society, a high IQ society. And so, my IQ is so high that we are not just the regular geniuses we are the geniuses of the geniuses. So, Mensa is the top 2% of the brains in the world. And we are the 1% of that 2%. And that's hard for most people to even wrap their heads around. So, if you counted every person in the world and you took 2% of that, and then you take 1% of that 2%, that's how high our IQs are. And we're called the 99s because our IQ is, we are nine, 9.999 to infinity level of genius. And so, he would call me 99 and because he called me 99 and he didn't want to grow up and he always wanted to be Peter pan. so we were MAX and 99 and PETER PAN and WENDY.

Then there were other layers to me being called 99. Because then I would reply back to him. Okay. Max, because that's something for our generation as a show of a couple. So, we were always the other half of whatever couple we together thought were the coolest, best matched and most loving. Where each one adored each other. When it came to our looks and attraction for each other we were Batman and Wonder Woman to show our attractiveness to the rest of the world but we choose each other. I think he meant lots of women want Batman and Most Men want Wonder Woman but together we were a power couple that choose each other. So anytime he would try to leave, there were constant energy attacks, constant financial attacks. There were people who didn't know one another, each all in different states and countries around the world all seeing this. I was confused because Richard was single and had not told me of ex wives so I could not understand where they envy was except women in California from festivals that wanted me to close my practice because my client success rate was 100%.

You see, I've taught meditation and done life coaching joy therapy. Happiness Coach And I reprogram humans' brains and I specialize in the subconscious. I've travelled the world many years, So, I'm a profiler. Sometimes I teach meditation, sometimes relationship coach. I'm a classically trained fine artist, I cosplay, I write self-help books. Like I used to do a TV show, my own TV show and my own radio show, just all kinds of stuff to make the world a better place. To make people Happy.

And so, it was hard for me and the things I had to cut off because, I don't work like most people where I work. Richard told me I had to give up these things, And then I get paid for the time I just work. I work years ahead normally and change each quarter in what I'm doing.

And I had to stop doing all that, to go scout out the places. And I had to keep my promise not to start any new businesses, not to sign any new contract, not to delay us by Opening any stores or offices, and finally says Richard so that whenever he could figure it out, I would be ready. Then he called and said, he'd been working on it. And that's when he told me about an ex-wife and the things that were getting very difficult and him realizing that people weren't just stopping him in the physical world, but also in the spiritual world, he was having to change as a person. He said the threats he'd been dealing with had changed So, at first it was, if you leave, I'll take your money and the things you've put in our names. He the things he put in their names, they threatened to keep them, but he didn't put them in their names to give them to them.

He put them in their names as like a tax thing , things the wealthy do, and not having too much stuff in his name, but the agreement was they'd have to give it back so they didn't want to now because they loved Having his stuff, but once they had his stuff, they made it clear to him that they didn't love having him. They behaved and pretended to get his cash but never loved him. And so, the verbal abuse increased he had lived like that, and now that he had found me according to him and I was like, you know I don't know really what to say to this, but I guess you've already done it and you're divorced. And so that would've been helpful to me to know where all these energy attacks we're coming from. But what I did was I just started meditating, more having to people pray for us, Richard and Me. Now the three women made sense. You are a handful Richard three ex wives!

The King of Cups

So, by 2019, I had said, you know, maybe it's not going to happen. And I can't keep putting my life on hold because I am losing so much money and I was starting to Have the list of all the places I was like, I've done everything. And he said, no, you haven't, you need to give up your inventory and all your stuff, because where are we going to put it? So, make sure that you're not holding on stuff to do a business that you're not going to do anymore. So, make sure that. When I come, you've got your favorite stuff in two suitcases, and we'll just have to get new stuff as we figure that part out, because what you have to figure out the most is how to get me out of here.

And I said, you know what, what if you're lying? What if you're like just some Dude, living in your mom's basement, just making stuff up or, you know, that kind of thing to tease him. And he was like, you think I'm not trying to come.

And I was like, okay, I'm not saying that you're not trying 99. And he said something was going on with his company. And so. He had told them he changed his mind and he wasn't going to fight because he grew up fighting. He was going to not let their darkness win, every act trying to hold onto him, make him fight for more money to give up his place in the company. So, he decided to take less money to go and put the house on the market again. And so, the house went back on the market and then it didn't sell again. And then he called me and said that that week, no matter what we would at least get a chance to see each other again. So, he put he said he was, he put me on hold to see how he could arrange his schedule to come to California so that he could tell me his newest plan to leave Hawaii for us to be together.

He came back on the phone and told me my flight information to Hawaii.

He had to go to the trademark office that week so he flew me to him the next day.

And I said, okay. And then when he called back, and he said, my schedule has too much going on. So, I booked you a flight to come here and then I'll show you now, so that I would know he was really trying to sell the house and all that kind of stuff, and that I shouldn't give up on him or us and what he was trying to do and that I wasn't giving up my I life for a lie. But I was doing it for us and I said, okay. So, of course I would do that for us so he flew me there, made sure that I, you know, knew about the house 4140 Black Point Road.

I land in Oahu. First he took me to his grandmother's house. And to the park. Because before he mentioned, you know, the square footage, but then he, then I knew the address and all that kind of stuff. And the next day, I think property managers and buyers were supposed to 4140 Black Point Rd Honolulu, Hawaii. came and he got a hotel for us and then went to take Moose home and he then returned.

Called and said that moose had pooped all over the house and the buyers were coming. And so he would have to stay there and clean it up. Or we might be stuck again because of course they're not going to buy a house covered in dog poop. Richard returned to our room And at that point, some woman he knew that he had been in a relationship with and somebody else so some women had stolen money from him and someone else had been stealing money, cashed a blank check that he'd written them. So he wrote someone a blank check long ago and I think it was. I can't remember what he said, how much. I think it was but they'd just cashed this blank check. And so now some stuff had to be moved around and something was going on.

And of course he was very upset at the betrayal and he needed to go deal with that. And he wasn't feeling well. And so, he told me that he had to go to the urgent care and he left to go the urgent care. And then he called me back with a diagnosis. But each time, time and nonstop, there were constant energy attacks on his health, my health, his finances, my finances, my business.

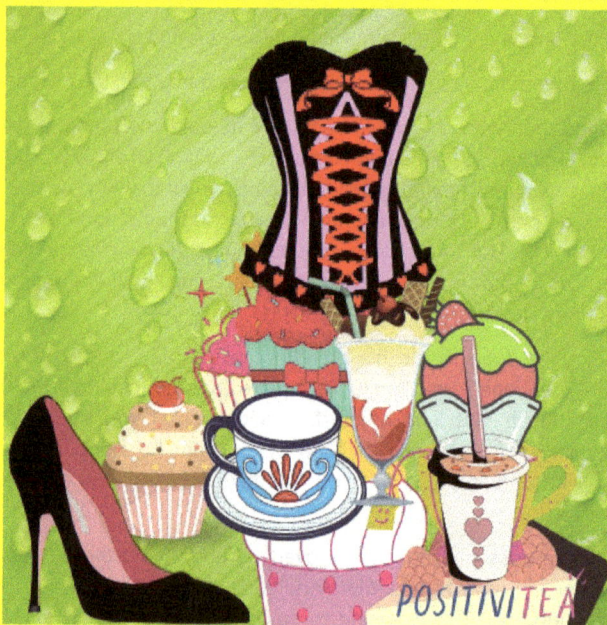

The Great Wave Artist Hokusai Let's Go On This Journey

And then threats kind of extorting to make him stay there. And he said, he'd already fallen for that for 17 years and he didn't want to die unhappy. So he was going to leave because he had decades of life ahead of him. But of course that was because he was Peter pan. And I was Wendy. So I figured Peter would pull off his plan, but the energy attacks continued the way Chinese medicine works is meridians flow.

And when negative energy is sent, it can stop the proper flow, which results in What we think of as physical illness. And then when we reset and clear the meridians it is fixed. So yeah, when I left Hawaii, we were all set and then he was leaving, no matter what, in a few days even if the house didn't sell, he was still leaving.

If he didn't get any money out of his company right away, he was still leaving. He was just leaving. And just, you know, to be able for us to look out for his kids from here California or wherever he decided we would be, but he wanted to be able to decide as we went along. And I've traveled all over the world so we were each and both ready.

So I was saying, I can be flexible in that and leave it up to you, because I feel great traveling and (have had a set travelling schedule for years). I said, I think we should stay close so that somewhere stationary for your kids. And that's when he said you don't understand what's really going on and you don't understand how it is for me here, but I have to get off this Island and you don't understand what I've been living with.

And so I said, okay, so he should have come to me in the next couple not few weeks, no more than two weeks. But instead when he came, he didn't tell me on the phone. He just called and told me he was there. He didn't even tell me he was coming to California to the Bay area. He just came and then he sent me a message and I was at church and I got the message after church because I always turn my phone off as most when they go to church.

And then that's when he told me Where he was and he wanted me to come to him so we could figure out what we're going to do next. And I said, okay. And what I didn't know is Jason had tried to commit suicide. And when I first got there, he was just shaking. He didn't, he wasn't his normal self at all.

He wasn't laughing or joking or he wasn't normally the Joker acts when He SEES Harlequin, I could tell he was trying to be casual, trying to be lighthearted, trying to be funny, but he was really nervous and I was trying to figure out why he was distraught. He was just broken and I reached for him as he walked towards me, was mumbling, I'm so glad you're here. What's wrong. And that's when he just collapsed into my arms when I took the second step into the door.

He literally physically collapsed. And said Jason and tried to commit suicide. And the police were called and all kinds of stuff like that. And I said, well, we'll have to just make sure we keep him safe. And he said, don't you understand how this happened And then I said, you know, I'll do a meditation. Get the answers.

Puddin couldn't talk, he needed to fill with light. Will it, usually Puddin's (Pet name for the Joker) Chi flows well, not that day. Two healings needed to take place. We can figure out what's going on. And he said, he knew, and that Jason was in the building down the hall or next door, he said, he's just right over there. And so that man, said I have to keep all the players on the field, he was the next room over or a couple rooms down. And then we were talking and he said he was going to take him, Jason.

go China and give him to the monks. So, somebody could watch him 24 hours a day because Richard said he was watching every window and every door and just trying to do everything Jason wanted or needed so that he wouldn't die. And that we would wait. Until he could get Jason stable about six months to a year and we left it at that.

Richard and Jason would use my light and we would get him stable.

And then some 6 months later women try to call me and send me emails, pretending to be Richard, but they didn't have any code names. nor his written voice nor his educational style, so many bouts of Black magic to keep us apart.

Long before this So, Richard told me right around the time of his auntie's funeral when he had to go to China for an aunt's funeral that someone had stolen his phone and hacked into it. And he was saying , people were Spelling his food. I don't know I had to get Google, but basically, people around him had decided it would be better if he was dead because then they could have all of his money instead of him leaving them and of course, taking some of his money with him and being owed some. So, while I was there in Honolulu, he went to the trademark office, but his phone had been stolen a couple of times, but the first time it happened was when his aunt's funeral and the hacker had, he said the data was compromised because he thought that I think it was the second time or the third time when the phone was stolen, that he just thought it was somebody just trying to steal a phone because of the value of the phone.

But the first time he said someone hacked into it and got the data, which was around the same time that I started getting calls. Women asking me basic stuff that were totally unrelated. You know, someone calling and saying is Bob there knowing that there's no Bob, and it's hard to explain to people when they call and think they're fooling you that people pay me for Spiritual at Church we call Prophecy and the world calls psychic abilities 8 I was born with.
And I knew something else was going on because the person, the great number of gifts I was born with, knew that the person knew that there was no Bob there.

That's what I knew the person calling didn't know anyone named Bob and they didn't know me. And so, I didn't know why else the call was happening. And it was 10 months before Richard told me his phone had been taken and the data was all compromised. So, he had me to look into secondary businesses, you know he was always coming up with a new plan so this time not stuff I would ever be involved in or would have thought of Right. But stuff that I could consult on. In the manner in which I consulted for stuff for wealthy private parties over the years.

But he wanted a business that wasn't attached to people who could hurt him from stuff he'd already done, use him for his money. So, he wanted something outside of Mytex, And so I thought of industries for him and despite my own dain for drugs because he loved green without seeds I researched a cannabis business for him and I remember he told me his phone was stolen again, and that he felt his illnesses were not natural.

Supernatural Meets The Blob

Again his Phone was hacked. Well, the phone was stolen and hacked into. He wanted me to know that he had experienced women who: Pretended to love him until he put them in a position to have control. And then they would let him know, they hated him. They became Very blatant and cruel with a lot of arguing and fighting and bickering and backstabbing and betrayals and adultery.

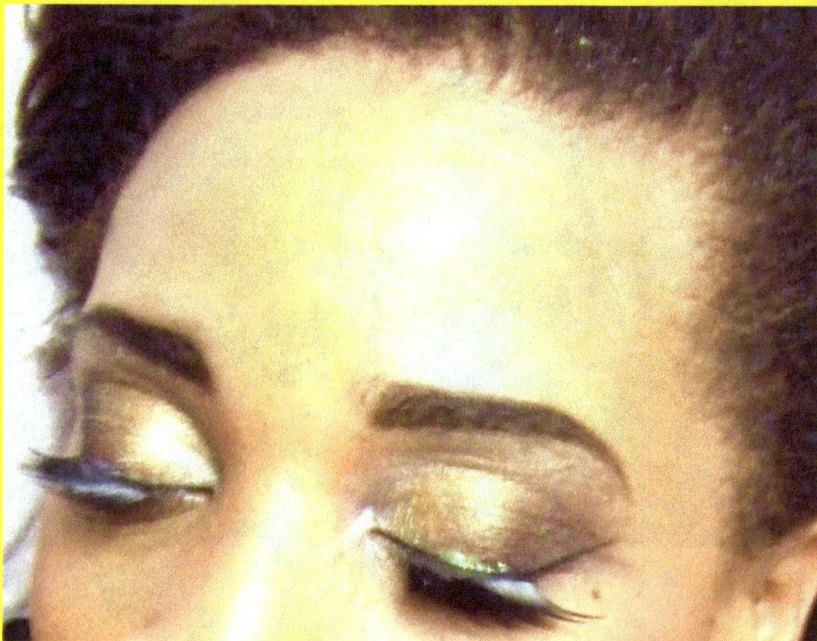

the Soul Interception of the Dream

A lucid dream is a dream that you don't initiate is mostly a spiritual attack.

Actually I have eight spiritual gifts and I've helped find a lot of missing children and help grownups' souls be free of misery and contamination. I'm also a teacher/Chi-Prana-Huna-Qi finished Chinese medicine school in 1997.

So, I had a dream that Richard was trying and he was trying to get everything together. I was confused my dreams don't usually include stuff people are trying to push through- instead just me and God. My dreams are always prophetic, what happens is you/I see stuff that happens later in the physical or answers to a question meaning I don't need just my dreams to tell me stuff spiritually, but this is a gift I was born with. Gift 6. And I was thinking, okay. Maybe I shouldn't listen to the girl who had said something to me at my conference hotel. I was doing a seminar and I was at a hotel and she said, someone was fighting so hard to get to me that they were bugging her, as soul, they were trying to get her to tell me stuff that I wouldn't listen to. I was born in California and we meditate a lot. And I did meditation and went to sleep. I always do a meditation and go to sleep. And so, I call it being putting myself in equipoise with GOD, which means my dreams are always prophetic because of the vibration and dimension I put myself into before I go to sleep. I don't have sleepless nights. And then after my dreams of and things that I needed to see or do or work on or help people, I saw Richard and there was a green and blue chest of drawers. That means a long rectangular box of drawers, Now we call almost everything a dresser, but not everything's a dresser. Furniture history is a part of architectural history, the furniture we use to store our clothes, they're named after the old luggage we used to carry before we had airplanes, cabinets and closets built into the walls of our house. Anyway this dream was that detailed and Richard had worked hard taking care of everything he needed for his plan, each being represented by a different drawer and was sliding in the last drawer. This was in 2018 so I didn't know that he had so much to handle.

So just as everything's not a dresser every dream is not just a dream. As a matter of fact most dreams or not just dreams. So anyway, I saw Richard and this dream. And it was blues and purples and greens that were bright and he was arranging everything. And he said, I've only got one more thing to do. Look. And as he put in the last drawer as all the other drawers were in place. So that meant Everything was in place and he was finished.

And then when he put the drawer in which meant he was finished. And as he did that, I saw a black-eyed creature, a very pale skin, looked like a woman, but a female of a creature and the eyes were black. And then it/she said, You., I killed your daddy and I was just shocked, that's so freaking weird because number one, it just came after I saw Richard do this last thing, which meant he, he was coming and then number two, it was weird because I was raised to be, yeah, feminist, I literally was raised by A feminist mother who surrounded me by feminists and feminist education.

So, my subconscious is feminist so I didn't know anyone else that that dream could apply to other than Richard, because Richard has a funny personality. Once early on he asked me to call him daddy to give me a hard time, for I am probably the only woman he knew he would never get to do that. And where, and when and... I would say, you could just say, daddy he'd say, I'm like, I could just, I got it, but I won't. And so, it became this game that he was more enticed and happier and intrigued to try to get me to call him daddy. This had probably been easy for him to probably tons of women throughout his 24 years of being a partying Playboy. He'd explain and tell me stories of these old party days.

Women chose to either to please him to get money or gifts or some kind of manipulation or their mindset was that's the role to play.

And as a feminist, I would never voice or experience being impatient because he was making things, care of things that were serious, things that were important to him. Even though I didn't know the details of what those things were, it is more my personality to work to make the world a better place, not worry about everything the workaholic I'm dating is doing. I figure they are doing things they need to do.

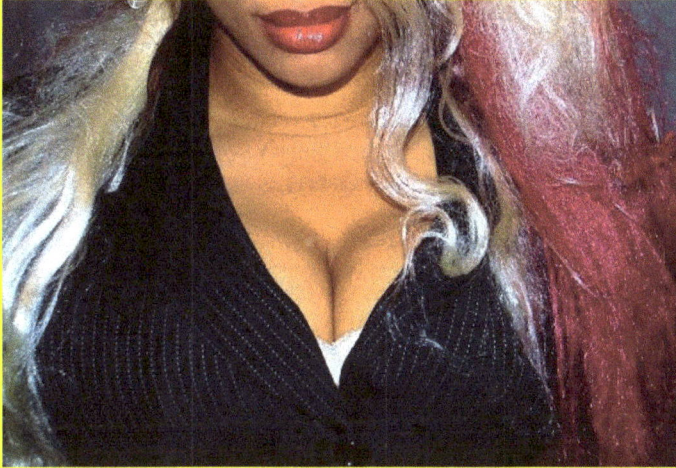

His stubbornness probably made him waste a year it was that first year.

Richard would also tell me stories, of him growing up.

Because he'd grown up in a ghetto and He never wanted to have to go back there, but because he had that desperate childhood in his subconscious, he didn't want people to take from him things that his charm and his personality made possible. Of course. Yes, because his stubbornness of they're not going to do this to me. I shouldn't have put anyone in a position to be able to do this to me. So, I'm going to find a way. And so, he decided he's going to find a way. And I, my part was to, you know, close my business and my truck, give up my life, show that I was actively giving up the things that weren't the same, like monetary very well, but well is it's relative. It's a very Scorpio thing.

It's more of a practicum. If you only have the illusion of well, meaning you have a lot of money, but you have no health or you have a lot of money and You have no joy. You have a lot of money and you're surrounded by no one you can trust. Then you know that you're not wealthy. And very often there will be someone who has nothing but love. Wealth includes all of the latter attributes.

Some component, right? So, they might not have all 8 or the four cores that we can see that we usually acknowledge. Because if you have at least three, you could get through life, at least feeling that you're happy. But if you only have the one and you're surrounded by horrible vibrations of backstabbing and gold digging and betrayal and gossips and mannequin fake hearts, And Richard used to use this song from when he was young called backstabbers. And if they hadn't attacked me I would have thought maybe he was exaggerating. Wei Ming. I loved Wei Ming such a beautiful name. He was usually Max through.

You know, no matter how much money you have, if you're surrounded by backstabbers or nobody real, you're surrounded by misery. So, you can't even enjoy what you have. Your eyes never twinkle. Your soul gets darker. Your heart has no light and few blessings flowing to it. Until sometimes you are just looking for someplace that you have joy in one aspect, and then you go to the next aspect of your life. And the joy is still not there either until sometimes you find a mannequin, that's what we call it in my classes. And the mannequin pretends to be a real girl. But she does everything you want. And I don't believe that he was like a total Playboy in the normal sense of the word, because he would say things like I haven't had sex like that in years. And so generally, if you're just a lying cheater he wouldn't need to say that.

And if that's all you care about then you wouldn't notice that your sex was empty so that you're happy when it's deeper. It's kind of a seminar I used to teach. I still teach it once in a while, but not right now. Of course.

Where I call it the milkshake! where some guys are parasites and what they do is they find a woman that has a lot of light, joy, happiness, peace, you know, meaning inner harmony fortune meridians.

And they exude this energy that light and good kind hearts pour forth sometimes people just want to drink up. Well, most people are gravitated to Snow White, Golden Hearts. They gravitate to that person because they can just be in the energy field. They can be in an environment sitting near you, it's the energy that your Golden

Hearts soul gifts out by trying to have part of itself or being in the body. So the soul is who we are eternally. I grew up in California and I grew up in church. So those of you who laugh because we say vibe that's on you because you flock to California because so many of us focus on the vibe whether you know that or not, just similar to Snow White , they are gravitated to our vibe. They're magnetically pulled, Just the goodness. No manipulation. Just the goodness. Right you just feel better because they are there.

So, the ones that are parasites, the ones who know they are villains, they eat women. So, they come into your life in order to drain and use your light and suck it dry. And then now you think of a milkshake. That's why we called this The MILKSHAKE part at a seminar and the milkshake class and the milkshake courses, because they suck up your light, your health, your wealth, your joy, your luck, your light is attached to those things. And light brings those things. Your light energy is God's light. Right. Yes! to think anybody's light will do it.

So, they find the brightest glowing woman and they drain her until she becomes like the milkshake. And when they get to that point where there's no more, they're going to hear that noise for those of you who have ever had a milkshake. There's a noise. Okay. That little zwwww where you've got that last bit. Well, what happens is when you've got that last bit, they know that sound is coming because because your straw has hit the bottom they've done it to so many women, they find the next woman and they start to drain her because the current milkshake is already so drained.

She doesn't look how she looked when she met him, because she's been being his food source, his light source. No! you got it. And being drained by the parasite. So, the parasite looks for a new woman, starts draining her.

Now they're also vampiric type couples. And we see that in the news, right? Where a wife sends her husband to go cheat so they can steal or drain light from others because in the couple both of them are so incredibly dark and parasitic.

That even when they have sex, there's no energy or light that comes through. There is nothing that brightens them. Their house is the reason a Mausoleum. Okay. So, it's like we have a class for that and it's, a class I still do if you live in a Mausoleum. And if you bought a mannequin, it's pretty sure. That you live in a Mausoleum, it may be decorated, but it's cold. The empty and the Hollow are different because the empty is a place where they could and should be love but no love is present thus the thing is vibrationally cold. Whereas a Hollow is a non-apparently Dark Soul there is something there but it's dark and nothing else the inside of a mannequin.

The Empty

And the energy is usually dead stone cold. Okay. And the reason that I was shown in my meditation when I was praying to God, what to do. And people need these classes cause you keep getting more and more clients that are living in Mausoleums with Mannequin.

And then I realized one of the mausoleums is different.

They're all cold because usually because there's so much stone and the richer ones are the houses that hold men trapped by mannequins. You know demonic women casting spells, and torturing them and doing all kinds of stuff to make them virtually a puppet whose money they're stealing. And vampires the joy their wealth should be bringing them,

It's like they need the puppet in place. So, the puppet continues to make money, but they need the puppet to be controlled so they can abuse the money. So, they live in the mausoleum and architecturally, they're built just like a lot of houses that those men are living in where there's a lot of windows. So, there's an illusion of light

Illusion of Light Alice

So, I'm a scientist, essentially. I shouldn't even say essentially, I am a member of Mensa. That's a high IQ International Genius Society. And all my childhood and most of adulthood in labs and on think tanks, so, although I was born with six psychic gifts that I use and two gifts I don't use, you know, the world would call them psychic gifts, they've been tested in labs. I would call it gifts from God. But instead I call them by their lab and university common names, but that's because I'm such a scientist. I prefer and trust when spiritual skills are proven.

I even studied the psychic world through books and the scientific method. Proof Is when you do a certain method and your results are accurate and how universities did study testing and growing my gifts and from childhood developing them and learning how to have complete control of them. And as a grown up with mastery teaching others how to, and also debunking misnomer we have about certain types of psychic gifts and abilities.

And in Chinese Medicine school, I just learned better, just focus on energy and your gifts flow as they should. And so, I became like an orchestra of healing and clairvoyance and clairaudience and psychometry and telepathy and empathy and telekinesis. So, as that was happening, I check time lines would reach branding ideas for my clients. Find missing children and help stop villains, erase trauma and manifest happiness.

So My first two years, I would put my fingers on their pulse. That's how you check the meridians, how you try to figure out scientifically which meridian is "off", how the Chi is flowing or not flowing. But usually one meridian is stealing from another. But eventually, you can do it intuitively, right? Eventually, Mastery maybe it'll take some lifetimes for some people, or maybe some people have had so many lifetimes doing a certain type of trait a brilliance in painting, medicine or some other art, right.

It's the same for Chinese medicine, holistic medicine in general, Western medicine that you're better at it than most you're abnormally better supernaturally, better at it.

Probably done it a few lifetimes. Yeah. And what I learned is I would do a small class and someone would turn it into a book, then I would reach for the Meridian, as I would reach for the Meridian I could feel the energy. And I thought it was God, of course. And it is God because that's the only energy that I'm willing to entertain, you know, especially back then. So, I would touch my client and they would fall asleep as soon as (97 Chinese Medicine School) I touched them and I'd work on the Meridian and I'll balance and time after time a woman who had suffered 20 years she'd go home healed of it all.

Then the next client will wake up and they would ask when I was going to start working and I would have them look at the clock. Check your phone, things to verify time passing, not a lot of clocks on a Chinese medicine office for that. For them to realize I already had worked on them or they would cry the entire time and tell me the most horrible stories of incest and abuse that they had lived through and now they knew that all of that was gone.

So, I found Chinese medicine because my grandfather was in the World Wars. And so I grew up visiting my grandparents they lived 3 blocks away, you know, three-story home, super long driveway and roses just as the gardener took care of at our house. But in their house there would be things he brought back for my grandmother or brought for himself from places his ship went. And so I was always taught a love and respect for Asian cultures. And my parents taught me no racism meaning they put a lot of energy to make sure don't teach me stereotypes about anybody nothing but the wonderful accomplishments to believe about everybody. Nor was I raised with any stereotypes that anybody might believe about me. It's a wonderful to see the world. That is why I am so energetically Alice. (In Wonderland).

World Wars They only taught me was to stop the Holocaust

And I grew up with my parents, taking me to Chinatown, to shop and theatre, and the museums and the Japanese tea garden and they let me always talk to the geisha (They gave me beautiful Geisha dolls when I was little long before I ever met a Geisha). I studied geisha for 30 years, the history and what I thought was everything.

Now, of course, I was a child, so they never mentioned the sex part of any of it. And they protected me, shielded me. To this day Chinatown is one of my favorite places in the world. I love KOI to this day spending 1000s of days sitting next to Koi ponds my favorite place to meditate from 22 years of being in TeaGardens.

My entire family and my parents protected me.

Like my parents literally raised me with no racism, no stereotypes. And not to judge. About anyone, no knowledge of the horrible things that Soul has done to one another in history. And when I say that, I mean if it wasn't on a movie or the news, I would never have known it existed. And as a child, I didn't watch the news unless I was sitting with my grandfather because of course, it was his generation of the forties -1954, After Pearl Harbor to be a good citizen, watch the news with the news reels. Movies didn't used to have previous they had newsreels so you watch the news before a movie when you went to the theater. Those are the people that raised me. Everyone knew about my gifts because I was born with them. But even better that they supported me, even church.

And so that transferred in their subconscious to always watch the news to be a good citizen. They taught me always to protect the constitution and be a good citizen. Be a good person. Don't lie, don't cheat, don't steal, and don't sell your soul. Even, I have an ex who's an extremely bad person. And he used to try to get me to be a bad person with him by saying your moral compass is too high.

And I would say, I don't even know what that means. And he'd say yes, because to you, that's the only way to be. And you don't judge other people, but you'll never change. You'll never sell out. You'll never sell yourself and you'll never betray people. And that's why he loved me and would giggle and melt his little evil heart.

I didn't know he was evil for two years

Right. But he was raised to be evil, so, he knew people and understood possible motives. I, as a doctor, specialized in the brain. As a psychic I'm a master but by my choice specialized in not looking into people's space without permission. I'm a master at the subconscious taking trauma out of it, putting good things in it,

Profiling and remote viewing, how to reprogram it, how to clean it and heal it. So, The Brain.

I didn't realize energetically there were people who put negativity in other people on purpose because I had spent nine years or really eight because by the ninth year after nearly two decades classes and being Happiness coach I was starting to figure it out a little bit, removing negative energy that was put there on purpose. But I had quantified that I was removing blocks in Chi that were locked in by traumatic moments.

And I hadn't realized that there were people who literally would use their Chi or the energy in the world or the energy that they could pull to harm others.
That's what you don't see when we do Tai Chi, we're pulling and releasing energy. The old people always put me in the middle.

Miracles Signs and Wonders each wondering how us meeting was orchestrated
GRACE AND FAVOR

Both hoping the other truly liked our true selves and we got confirmation from the light and the dark. Dark to keep us apart sending fake messages neither of us would remember sending. Knowing each of were different than the norm and had to keep erasing filters not holding the other responsible for doubts we knew were not true. Something wanted us to not trust each other's motives, but they were based on stuff we secretly had already told the other that they people trying telepathy they didn't know were not true for us. An actual example of sending him messages claiming I didn't want him anymore for something they didn't like about him but he knew I adored about him or was one of my favorite parts. And for the orchestrated way we met and Master Teachers around the world announcing his arrival this meeting for two years. We didn't try to meet each other.

For some reason like some weird puzzle put together by the universe Miracle Supernatural movie level We instantly each just have this weird level of attraction automatic love and Trust for one another and of course as a Scorpio "Scorpio stressed" and I go through the world trusting everyone until you do something then I never trust you again, so our personalities neither were not really ones where you just you know love at first sight fall in love trust and 1st off the bat want to be with them talk to them all the time always will save always at ease and laugh and play but that's how we treated one another from second day that we met I was jeez what the heck is wrong with me and then by the end of the first week he was a Non-Stop Chatterbox because we both just were safe and fine and almost We believe that it was somebody on the planet we actually could trust with our true selves. Well, I think by the time I was 25 when I started taking Tai Chi seriously doing Tai Chi with the elders in Chinatown. It's always so fun because I take my sword they always put me in the middle and then each one teaches you a bunch of little things. So, people pulling energy. I thought we pull in the good God wants us to have and release anything that would make us, you know, not Godlike. I learned from friends Apparently, there are people who are just pulling negative energy so they can make a ball of it so they can put it in the lives of people they envy or people that are racist against.

That was kind of shocking to find out, but I was already with a strong practice that when I found that out and I was so sad and one by one, the Feng Shui Masters in China confirmed it. The souls doing attacks and I call it not remembering who they were meant to be. And being so covered in negativity that they were polluted and they were thereby polluting other souls according to the Elders they said of the attackers the buddhist Nuns saw them and said are your opposite almost pure hate and envy just because your vibration is too high.

So, instead of the envious asking me how I got there or how I can teach them to do it too, they said I'm going to pollute you so that you can be dirty like me. What?. Other people were being told by GOD, they understood on a more demonic level that if they put negative energy in your space, maybe they would muddy up the water or tar up your journey.

They do it so, it would be harder to get to your goal, your blessing, even if you didn't know, your soul has a goal and the universe has goals. And so they put stuff in your way that's not supposed to be there. So, they try to get you to be as if it was a

Hollywood movie or in the theater, and for movie sets there are those little X's on the floor and that's your mark, and you're supposed to stand there when you are ready.

That's what you do for your blessing: the Universe does things to place you in alignment a vibration being that little X on a Hollywood movie shoot you stand on the X, get navigated to the X lines up with someone else and get your blessing.

Waves and dolphins

So, that's kind of what a curse is. It turns out that a curse is energy that's not yours trying to disrupt your frequency or giving you physical or mental illnesses. So, let's say you're a telepath. That means you can hear other souls and other energetic beings communicate with you. And when I say energetic beings, beings have different frequencies. I mean one example would be the dolphin, one time I was parasailing and I just loved it I was over the ocean and as I just Open my heart and I was just loving it and flying over the ocean. The dolphins kind of felt it whenever I'm on the water, If I'm catamaraning, scuba diving or parasailing. Whether I'm in Monaco, Hawaii, California, or Cape Cod.

On my TV show When you hit that Mark that's when you start talking or when you're on that Mark that's when, as a broadcaster, I do my presentation or do an expose.
So, with Chinese medicine, the acupressure points are, you hit that Mark and all that you are flows and helps that person remember all of who they truly are and removes everything that's not them.
California It doesn't matter where I am in the world the dolphins come and I'm always so happy. Well in California, they'll even swim along the shore whenever sitting at the beach.

I Don't just have Snow White Energy I also have the Cinderella Energy.
The other day I had a meeting and the meeting was about two or three hours long and the dolphins would just swam one direction, going left, you know, and as soon as I lost a visual view of them, the dolphins would kind of turn back around. So, they would swim probably about a mile across the horizon and not out towards the sun,

but across, along the shore beach, and then they would turn around and go back the other way. And they did that the entire three-hour meeting so I got to see them the whole time, which was wonderful. Richard's questions especially early on were always hilarious.

you have to know anyone pretty much sleep with one eye open and are some of them are psychically spiritually naturally gifted people and will never tell you and will never admit it but they run your lies not true cuz it's more than spidey sense if they are not arachnid they are street smart and spiritually smart to ask you a series of questions usually crazy where what seems to be stupid questions because they're testing at most points are you going to lie never be dumb enough to lie to a Scorpio no matter what you've done because they're going to know that you're lying. And when they know you're lying they're not going to tell you, they're not going to tell you they know you're lying they'll just feel mawhh I caught you so they know who you are for the rest of your freaking life

Tea Cups

But that day I was parasailing and I was in Hawaii and The dolphins came in. The whole school of dolphins were right under me and wherever the boat went, they swam along.

So if boat turned, we turned, they turned. And so they stayed under me so long that the driver of the boat realized it. So being the master at parasailing that he is, he adjusted the boat's speed to land me right in the school of dolphins. So yes, I have swum with the dolphins a lot. Although I don't believe that you should pay to swim with dolphins. I do believe that it's bad for the dolphins to be used in that way. It's too many people and their vibe and people get healed when dolphins are present. People get healed by the fact that dolphins or whales, different types of sea life are present. But if we put too many people, the animals don't have time to recover their own vibration after cleaning your funky low human vibe and they have your negativity.

Funny Cups 3 D Abundance and Happiness

But when I catamaran I am excited sitting and watching through the net and to sit on the net so that of course I can meditate.

So I when catamaraning the Dolphin swim along under the net while I sit on the net and while parasailing Dolphin swim under me as I fly overhead following my flight pattern and half way through I landing from the sky in my gear swimming with those same dolphins in the deep open ocean off Honolulu. And then of course he was a master so he just sped the boat up. And I went back up into the air and finished my parasailing day.

And so that I can watch what's in the ocean as we're speeding by. So, I always lay or sit on the net. And I was doing that when the dolphin came and I was oh, Hey, now it doesn't only happen with dolphins. It is energetically what I allow. I don't allow the whales to do it anymore because it's one thing when you go whale watching and you think, Oh, this is going to be so fabulous and everybody goes whale watching. It's another thing when you're me and you just open your heart and you wish to fill the whales. They can feel that much love. And so I was in a boat and, whale-watching expedition with others and the next thing we knew, there were eight whales. They were bigger than the boat each whale.

And so what they did was they made a circle around the boat. Six whales inner circle and two on the outer edges at different ends of the circle. And they swam in a circle around the boat, you know, feeling the love, drinking, the light, that kind of thing. And it was both scary And Exhilarating. It was so cool. It really was. That's how it is for some in times if you fall in love with someone who has a lower vibration than you. Either by energy, other people put there, or their own energy or the hopelessness that they have fallen into because of being constantly attacked or controlled or manipulated with other people's negative dark or dead energy. And you're such a bright light and they love you, but it's almost as he was a vampire trying to look into the sunlight, but they're determined because they know they've been trapped in a dungeon so long. So, they transform and let the sunlight burn off it of them. The things that have been keeping them dark.

Light

Now, if they are a dark person, meaning they were brought up to be dark. They, as a child, things were put in them to help them be dark because it's just what they do, you should never judge a soul for who they are. I'm not saying hanging out with people who are trying to harm you, but I am saying you can't just be telling people, I'm light, you're dark so I'm better. You can, a matter of fact, that would show a huge lack of consciousness, the same way that people say, Oh, I'm woke. And then they gossip and they're mean, or they're arrogant. In one instance one time a spiritual teacher, he locked himself out of the car after giving us hours and hours of lectures about him focusing on sexual energy instead of love energy and people were taking classes so they could follow his system.

And I was there with a client and she was working on a course to empower women, to accept their bodies. And so, I was coaching her through that and she'd been doing it, she needed me so she could focus more on the energetic part instead of the biological body part and then just tell them, they'll feel it. So, that's why she was my client.

And so, I needed to see one of her teachers and understand that market. And so, I was there. And I kept saying this guy is so weird vibrationally, right? What he was saying, from a stage built in his home, didn't match the vibe I could feel in him and see and specialize in his subconscious, the verbiage, the words he was using, not just the syntax, but the verbiage showed that he was not just insincere, but he was recruiting to manipulate.

But I couldn't figure out what, because I didn't look into his space without permission. I prefer to keep my energy high, as opposed to violations of spiritual laws, and look in people's space without permission. And there are some people who believe you should look in everybody's space, cause you never know what they're up to, but those people's vibes never reach a certain height because they do that.

That guru from above yelled, screamed, cursed and beat his car trying to get in when he locked himself out.

Wealth of Light

If you want to know someone's vibe, ask God, now God might not tell you their vibe. He'll just tell you if he should be there or not. And I remember when I met Richard, I would get confirmation from God that no matter what I saw, no matter what I felt, God had put him there and he had. God had given me this kind of security, not a security net, but a security network and door of memories so that I would always know, this is not someone who walked up to you while you were cosplaying for charity or in costume for a book, or you were at a ball or a conference, or he said, this is. I orchestrated this.

And then I'd remember I had two brand new bedding sets on my bed and I never told Richard this, but I always have ten plus years have a practice of marrying two sets of bedding on my bed, so it's more cushy, more etheric, more fairy tale. And just like a fairytale princess, I hang things from the ceiling over my bed and flowers and netting, just beautiful. As if the Fairies and Angels worked together and must have made it. And my bed was perfect complete, you know there's a special feeling when your bed gets complete, your batting and the decorations and you know it, you can feel it in your heart. Weeks before we met.

Now I looked at my bed. It was almost a few days. No more than that. I think it was two days when I was so happy with my new design I was happy every time I walked into my room (it had been 20 years since I had given up my hospitality high end design business from part of my undergraduate degree) I had just renewed my designers association membership and satisfied my bed's complete I was going to have fun with my new agency. I'd found the perfect of every pillow and right price. And I don't like tons of pillows I like bedrooms for sex and sleeping. I don't work in a hotel, so I don't think part of my going to bed should be me having to take off 10 or 18 pillows.

And take them off my bed every night to be able to get into bed. And then when I make up my bed in the morning, I've got to put all that crap back on in a special arrangement. I don't think that that is healthy living and it's definitely not for the joy of soul. We used to use that trademark. We still do sometimes, but it's a company segment that I started when I began to teach in the desert. So, I told myself I was in my loft and I couldn't believe it. I was knowing, it's so beautiful. It's so gorgeous. Every time I see it, I just divinely filled with joy and love. It's so wonderful. I love my love 3 walls of windows I could watch fireworks on the 4th of July down one end of the city of tech billionaires, the neighboring Town, switch windows to the other side of city and never leave my leave gorgeous setup, I sometimes quirkily choose to say, "add cilantro". My bed is finished. And then I had a spare new bedding in the closet right.

I was raised to take care of my husband, take care of my house, cooking clean and decorate my house and make things repair things very lucky. Always be prepared. It's as in the 1940s, 1950s housewife way. So, brand new bedding set in the package in the closet, two brand new beddings on my bed and then …

God said the day after I celebrated my home was complete that I woke up and he was like, you need to go buy new bedding. And I was just , what? What why Lord that's brand new, that's brand new, that's spare and the closet is full. So why do I need to go buy new bedding? And I was thinking, wait a minute. When do I negotiate with God? I just do what he says.

So, I got dressed. And instead of asking why I asked where, where to go, Lord, where do I need to go? So he said I had to go to Ross and I don't really shop at Ross, I hate that place: terrible thieves cashiers doing scams with credit card on customers cards, horrid customer service, and just so boring selection. AND I DON'T LIKE SPORT SHOPPING-I'm like a dude- I hate shopping for no reason I don't enjoy shopping because I lack something interesting to do with my day. I don't shop needlessly, I think I hadn't been to a Ross in maybe 10 or 15 years nor had I 10 or 15 years ago, and even then I'd not gone to a Ross more than once. And usually, it was, I was at a conference and they were the closest store to the convention center and I would go to get a pair of flats so that I would get out of my stilettos. Because I used to just wear pencil skirts and suits all the time now mostly just very beautiful dresses.

With stilettos. And at a conference you need to walk for eight or 10 hours and talk to thousands and thousands of people. And one of the conferences I attend is 180,000 people. So, I'm in pretty good control of my empathic abilities because otherwise, most empaths don't want to be around 50 people let alone 180,000 people. But I went to Ross like, okay, God said, go to Ross. So I tell Siri, find Ross because I have no idea where it is. And I get to the Ross that I pushed
I get there and God was like dude, this is the wrong Ross. And I was just , geez, Louise, you could have said that. Right.
Because that's, how I talk to God.
That's how we communicate. I just talked to him everyday since age 5, all day long. And what I should have done was said, which one, because even if people Want me to teach them how to use their spiritual gifts I used all gifts to connect to God Therefore I know different spiritual types of tools. I enjoy the physical world. They can gather tools and use the tools while they're developing their connection with God.

This time as I sat in the Ross parking lot I've learned when I pulled up the directions from Siri, ask, which one. If I had asked God which Ross in first place I would have been at the right one. It was not God's fault. So I opened Siri again, said find Ross and then I asked God which Ross and I pushed it. And I went to that Ross and it was another 25, 30-minute drive. And I went there because of course there was no Ross near my house and that meant huff, Okay, fine. Now I'm doing what God tells me. I'm going to be at the right place. It must be somebody who needs help or an elder with some wisdom or, you know, a little baby that their soul needs the blessing to be on their right road.

Or God wouldn't send me there. So I go to Ross and as I'm walking by comforter sets my psychometry just pops up, just touches bedding and God's like, that's yours. And I was happily surprised, Oh, it's perfect.I love it. I love it. I lived in Paris for years. And so this bedding reminded me of that and it had kind of my personality, but it was black. I don't like dark bedding.

So it was, that was also kind of weird because normally I wouldn't buy black. As I always plan my bedroom, very bright and lovely, but it was so beautiful that I bought it. And plus, you know, God said as the right one, my arm popped up, psychometry was right, this is yours.

I have to use it the new comforter it needs some stuff to go with it so it can be all Parisian and cutie patootie, not American Parisian, but me living in Paris. So, I get home and I was done, Oh my goodness what a pain in the butt day, I can't believe I had to drive so much today to go get this bedding And so as I was just about to pop the bedding in my closet hopefully, I was wherever you needed me Lord. And I talked to the people you that needed me to talk to them and I heard the souls that needed to talk to me.

When I laid face up atop my bed smiled closed my eyes And then I heard you need to wash the bedding. I opened my left eye what? really..And then I was worried for the first time in my life, okay, maybe it's NOT God, because I worked really hard for it to always be God and, you know, worked on a lot like discernment and never taking shortcuts and things of any other nature. As far as you know, well, no, right? No shortcuts, no deals.

Me and God. So I was of course giving in, okay, Lord, I never wash my bedding. I never, ever once in my life wash new bedding, I put it on my bed. I figured it's coming from a factory. So I wash it after it's mine and on my bed. Right. But I don't usually wash it before I use it. So, I put it in the washing machine and. I put away the rest of my things in my house while, you know, the washers going and the washer stops and I go to put it in the dryer and I always shake out blankets. Right. Cause I'm a trained designer/costumer, which is one of my undergraduate degrees. And so, I shake it out and I realized that there's a blank circle in the center of this comforter that was not there before that the comforter was fully covered print now is was not covered.

And the print that it was covered in has washed off literally completely. The only thing that was left were the edges. The edges had some print as if, to show proof that it had not just been a black comforter. Weird.

Okay. So, the comfort or had a print on it, the print on it was gone, the edges were there. I was about to meditate, okay, Lord now this really seems an interesting day. So, now I'm going to have to go back to the store and return this, that you just had me buy. And he said, no, you need to find the company, find the company that made it and call them and let them know what has happened. And I hung the comforter to dry. And I went to my room, did my meditation, read some through some spiritual materials and went to sleep and the next day I handled the to-do lists that day had given me.

Blue

I remember when ,Richard, he first started calling me. Richard Wei Ming Yee was so hilarious. He would call me and at first, I was puzzled with his casual nature in which he spoke to me like his chest eased. I'm very formal, I'm a multi-racial person. And the part of my ethnicities that controls my social behaviors tends to be quite formal. Like how I am around people. If I come to your home, how/what liberties I would take and not take very formal. I I'm the person who would just sit in the chair that you said, you know, I could sit in. The person who won't sit down until I'm invited to sit down that kind of thing. The person who says, may I use your restroom?

So, vernacular shows not just current social class, it tends to also show ancestral social classes. And a certain level of decorum has existed in my family since the 1700. So, I was raised, friendly, but not as casual. And I really just warmed up to him listening to him and he had to make it obvious that he was not calling about business and he did that, the first phone call and it never stopped. And there were times where it was like text or calls, you know, six times a day, 17 times a day, and the jokes and the stories and the laughing and the playing. It was like we were teenagers and he would say he had decided when he was young, that he was never getting old. He wasn't, he wasn't going to. And I had said my whole life that my numbers will change because you know, you don't want to die. But I would stay young and vibrant. Right. And he would say stuff , you're the girl version of me. And I would say, how do I have to be a shadow of you? Right. And he's joking, you have no shadow. Okay. So, it was very fun and delightful. And anytime that we spoke or saw each other that's what it was with the exception of I didn't know at the time, and maybe he knew, but he never mentioned it to me the mounting levels of energetic attacks to try to keep us apart, delay our lives, hurt our finances, attack and muddy up the waters.

Try to make him think stuff about me that I would never do, try to make me think stuff about him that he would never do and something else bring us having to come back to trust. And every time we did that, we literally got hit harder. With energetic attacks as if that would have worked on everybody else. Why didn't it work on either of you let us see, you know, attack you more, hit you with more stuff, more things. So, people often will hit us as humans, souls, and the bodies that we're wearing as costumes. And then we call ourselves humans when we are Soul and so much more. Infinite beings, right. That they want you not to remember that and the way to do that is to put thoughts situations in Greek Mythology Tales.
Those girls in Hawaii made me realize some people have no heart. They were EMPTY mannequin.
I should say when I say you I mean the informal you, not the personal you, cause there are people they can't feel as they've been hurt so bad or they are so dark or they're mannequin. A mannequin would only do that to manipulate. The informal "you" = means all people.
I'm a bibliophile, so I'm just going to, I'm not going to assume everybody knows Greek mythology. But in Greek mythology, there were things set up to keep you so enticed, having so much fun that you forgot to finish the part of your quest. Or destroy you before you can do your life changing and get reward. So like a video game we have chances to use gifts along the way achieving the quest.
Using my gifts is natural, people don't see it. That's happened to me at libraries for books, you know, also I use it when, psychometry is not just touching stuff. It is a

magnetic pole to touch something. It also can be when you touch something, you may see visuals of a missing kid so have a picture of where they are. So you look at, or you touch the photo you're provided, and then I get the audio-visuals. You will get the visuals of where they are, where's the body, or where's the child. And then that helps the parents and the police find and give the parents whatever peace they might need.

Or we help recover the living child who's lost in a forest, so it's a nice gift to have, but you don't want to touch some things and not touch everybody. Some property and items: things and Souls have super negative energy.

The World So I didn't need California people showing up like the 3 Billy Goats Gruff

And so, when people have no light because they can't decorate they would use a picture they found somewhere else because not even enough light comes from their soul for them to know where to put flowers. So, usually everything's dry around them.

The feng shui master helped me a lot. There was a man and two women. They thought that it was amazing that they could see me and that I refused to look into people's space without permission because according to them, that's when you need to look the most, the people that don't want you to look. They thought that it also made me such a natural at what I did because it just continued to make my abilities increase because they were never tainted. People try to taint you, try to pollute your space but that's them using their energy and putting it in your space. That doesn't make it your energy. It just may kind of block or hinder your energy a little bit or sometimes a lot. But your choice, everything is a choice. Not looking was a choice that at this point I don't know if it's good or detrimental. I think it's a combo of both, more detrimental than good.

My beloved Hawaii - and I as SNOW WHITE: WOMEN WHO ARE JEALOUS WILL TRY TO DESTROY YOUR LIFE

But I do know when you're in a position to look and you choose not to look you say something to the universe about the vibration and the realm in which you're willing to take messages from. That, in turn, helps your people that you're there to help. I believe we all have multiple soul families and that we have them for different reasons. As we grow, does it change? There are multiple ones we would fit in to serve different purposes in the universal plan, the game that's afoot. ALL Ohana. So, when you think of it that way, then there are people whose soul family doesn't have the rule of don't look, it's a violation of spiritual intrusion and their entire existence is looking, but they just look because they're trying to make sure you're not something there to harm them, but then there are other soul families who look to find your weaknesses or vulnerability so they can harm you. I, in the many years that I have done this over two decades, have met so many multimillionaire playboy friends of mine, who it is their nature to look because, for them, that data helps them get the woman or man they want.

I'd say it's probably two-thirds straight multimillionaire playboys and one-third gay multimillionaire playboys. There's a difference in what the different groups have told me, and they don't know each other. One group does because they are so cool. They all hang out together. Of course, the average alpha male doesn't have to seemingly hunt. Watch one of my commercials, my video and when I say commercial, you know, I've never advertised my business and in word of mouth my entire life. I've never paid for an advertisement. I don't believe that's the way the universe sends clients or people for me to help or projects that I'm supposed to work on or ways I'm supposed to change the world. My commercials are enjoyable, enlightening, reprogramming. You watch it, at one of my events you get your joy back and you're yelling and/or laughing, wow, I feel good. I don't even know why I feel good maybe I should watch another one of Mia's commercials. You say that kind of thing. So, the one, the fairytale series there's let me see, there are four, there's a fifth one that doesn't seem it's the fairy tale, but there are four where it's fairytales we all share in.

AMUSEMENT

A muse is the opposite of a mannequin. A muse is something that's so gorgeous and beautiful, so full of love, so full of knowledge, so full of that, it inspires you. Vibrationally you are healed and inspired to be the greatest you, or write a symphony or paint the Sistine chapel, or, you know, be da Vinci, be your style of da Vinci. So, the distractor-type things had been encountered before we met each other. Me, save the world helps survivors of incest. Right. Doing things he thought he was supposed to. They're not even girls, they're all mannequins. Right? So, what happens is a muse is a different thing.

That was me being on my soul's road helping people get onto their Soul's road, but I was never pursuing common things, especially being raised as a feminist. I never pursued things and men. I was raised hope they don't like you, but when you're very beautiful and then you're also sexy they kind of just bugged me since I was 12 and never stopped. And they never will. They will always flirt. but by age 13 going into labs I learned men were my favorite friends and favorite people to talk to. And I learned to just appreciate it. I think I was 34 Still being mistook for 25 or 22 to 25. So, I learned this is nice because this doesn't happen to all people. So, be gracious and say, thank you. But I would still turn down most men that asked me out and my ex-boyfriends can attest to that. So, when you're somebody that I say yes to you're very special and extremely special to me. So, Richard enjoyed that too. And I loved talking to him. I loved laughing and playing with him. I loved ...right. And I didn't know as much about things that were happening to him on an energetic level until year two. But I had given my word and happily in or to, being with him and him leaving and us living together and us having a life together so that as he put it, he'd be able to die happy, right.

For his soul to actually have peace and happiness and joy. Not outwardly, you know, faking it seemingly, but in his core, he wanted that. So, he knew some of the things that were happening to me because he was spying and I didn't know. But he was.

Because he had put me in harm's way. He had put me in danger spiritually. Once I started registering in his space, then I became something to attack because it was giving him joy and the mannequins wanted their puppets to be hopeless and suffering.

The alpha males, they're not in the forest, going, want some candy little girl. No, that's a few other friends I've had where, they know that they can manipulate some women with money and women wouldn't be attracted to them if they didn't have it. My friends that I've had, I guess 17 or 18 years, that just kinda gravitated towards me because of the workshops that I give. I always felt safer because all women are after them and I'm not chasing any guys and so it made them, cute playboys, make me just a part of the group. They all knew we have to just make sure everybody knows hands-off, don't talk to her., don't look at her, and then she(me) is surrounded by gentlemen. An audience for their stories, which also as a profiler as a doctor, as a member of Mensa, as a cosplay model who raises money to fight pedophiles or give to charities or make the world a better place, I enjoy immensely . The boys I call them, They entertain me and I love them adore them and understand them fully.

I love wearing a costume because I used to go to events where we wear a costume as part of a theme for a fundraiser for the events. But my love of comic books and anime and manga allowed me as a doctor to say, you know what, there are certain groups of people that nobody tries to help. Rich women, when they leave marriages sometimes become worse than you can imagine because in order to leave, they have to leave with nothing, but they need to leave in order to protect their children. So, if I put on a mermaid tail, use the images to do therapy, to help people be happy, sell them exclusively and give rights to charities. Use them without taking any money so that those people who there's no system set up in our government to help somebody I help. When you leave someone and there's Mercedes, and at this point, it would be Teslas and Lamborghini's and Maserati's in your name, and you go to a social office because you need to escape someone raping your kids or are trafficking them. They send you away because they think you must be crazy because you have this stuff in your name.

So, I figured out in 1997/2000 is when we became a company active in doing that, Medical Intuitive, a company that gave away everything we made or made products to give away. So literally I manufactured products to give away so that charities would have something they can sell to help these populations that there is no social answer for. So, we did that. So, all this time I'm surrounded by a very rich men, a very handsome rich men. For us, we each wanted people to be friends with that weren't always trying to get us to date them. Sometimes people don't understand that's a thing for beautiful people. We don't whine about it because it's a blessing. If you're beautiful. So, you should use it to make the world a better place. But we know that there are (what I named Mannequins) mannequins and viper women who use it to harm nice men who know that those girls would never date them. The spoken and unspoken rules, it used to be unspoken but the spoken deal is I give you money, you use me for my money, and you date me even though you're not attracted to me. That game changed long ago and no one told me.

Well, amongst my friends, we couldn't even fathom doing that because I always say you don't have to be handsome or cute to the world, but you do have to be handsome or cute to me because you need to love somebody and kissy face them. We started our Masterminds/classes because some men, want HAPPINESS to be a part of their life and want to be intimate and want to take care of them and adore them. So, I've dated models in Rome, but I've dated computer engineers. Being a computer engineer doesn't mean that you're not handsome because I think they're both cutie patootie but they're not alpha males. They're not sexy wolves (Alpha's) in a tux where women are chasing them and you know, throwing panties at them.

So, it's always been interesting to me when people don't value everyone as soul, EVERYONE. People that you like, people you don't like, people who have a super light soul, and people who may not. People that are dark. I think the problem is when we are not seeing someone correctly because they're really Iagos. You know, I believe that Shakespeare teaches about every soul we will ever meet in the world and I have taught that to more than 27,000 people.

Not Your Burger

So, let's go into the next house. The same world, we're still mostly on the planet earth, sometimes wishing we were somewhere else. When was the last time you were grateful for everything you have and told it? Thank you that I have such wonderful sewing machines. Thank you that I have such wonderful fabric. Thank you for the corsets I do have instead of hating on the 352 corsets I don't have on my wanting one corset for every day of the year. You just think, and if you do that every day, it will change your vibe. So, what do you think this part of our understanding dimensions and time and space and that everything is energy and how we just switch to a vibe? Some people think you've got to go be a monk. I love monks. I know a lot of monks so don't get me wrong, but most people don't think that they can be the best soul they can be because they don't have time to go live in the mountains for two or three years.

I've done it. I've literally done it where I went and lived in a desert for a year, or it was 17 months, which is more than a year, or the redwoods. I've done that or farmland. You see where you think you go into the middle of nature where nature is still king, queen, whatever you want to call nature. Nature is probably not calling itself non-binary. I think the way that I grew up ethnically the different parts of my DNA structure. Think of French, different parts of nature seem to be more male energy or more feminine energy. So, we attribute types of feelings that we feel when we are in nature, maybe perhaps with a certain gender.

So, when I say nature is king in all decks of cards, in all fairytales, the king is still above the queen. But no King is happy without the correct queen. Now we know in actual monarchies when there is a king, he's the top of the monarchy but when there is a queen who wasn't made queen by her king, she has a husband, but that husband is not called king. So, I mean, in that way, nature is king meaning nature the top boss of the hot sauce until we flip to energy. So, what we're doing when we go meditate in the desert, so we can hear God and all that kind of stuff and whatever people say, whatever you call God, "no judgments". I've never been in a state of judgment because I used not even be in judgment of me, but I never judge people I meet or people I'm friends with or date or love because I didn't want to lower my vibe and come from that JUDGEMENT placement on the grey scale.

I do what I can to keep my vibe high, which also includes not judging your vibe or anything you do. I used to say do what you want, as long as you don't eat babies. Then, of course, there was some stuff people were doing that I didn't know, humans even could do. So I needed to expand that list and still not go in judgment but say Universe here's some more stuff I don't want in my life. So, for years, we (my team) have taught and I still teach a class called **not your burger**. It has to do with being grateful for who you are but knowing who you think you would be a good love match with. Sometimes we're not grateful for the people we love. Sometimes we love people we shouldn't even be grateful for.

We love people that are harmful to us, but we want to stay in gratitude so for people were harming you to that, you say, thank you for the lesson. You can say thank you for coming and thank you for going, that kind of thing.

You can be saying, I'm glad you came into my life and I'm glad you're leaving it. You do that in neutral. You stay zero. So, when we are saying thank you to God, we're not just saying thank you for the good stuff. I'm saying, thank you for my wine bottle that I don't know why I don't have a top when the purpose... I don't drink wine so I buy the bottle so I can do something with it, and I pour the wine out or I gift it to a friend by buying a very beautiful bottle. Say thank you when it doesn't even make sense.

Now I don't have tons of friends because I don't like to take part in gossip and cruelty and silliness. I do have sorority sisters and as one ex pointed out, which I had never noticed, he observed and proudly commented, you don't hang around with them. You're not like other women and he just said it so casually. But as a man who spends most of his time studying women, I know he wasn't lying. I was just like; how did I not observe that?   He rightly explained, because you go to meetings with them and you do the stuff that your sorority does to make the world better, but you don't do stuff that women do that they are programmed for. So, he was completely right. I don't want to take part in gossiping. And I don't want to take part in talking about the spaghetti I cooked for dinner. Is that going to change the world? Okay, fine. We can talk about it, but I'm not going to talk about it out of just circumstance because I have nothing else to talk about. So, I tend to know women that that's not what they talk about and I tend to meet women who may be women that talk about that stuff. What I don't do is if let's say a woman goes to a class in college and then she learned some stuff about women's history she may get angry and call herself a feminist. This is the opposite to how I was raised and being raised by feminists and Baptist princesses, you could imagine, they made a hybrid without trying.

They thought they were going to win out. So, the Baptist princess figures they win out. The feminists thought they won out and the lesbian feminists thought they would for sure win out because they knew I was learning and applying everything they taught me as feminists, but I wasn't lesbian. Then they were sad, and stern, we don't know how to help you with some of this stuff, because we already told you who the enemy is. They weren't just lesbian feminists. They also didn't highly dress men, but they did teach me how to always value myself as a woman and understand how men have treated women throughout history so that I would know the possibilities and relationships. They had chosen same-sex relationships to prevent themselves from taking part in any of the relationship patterns historically men have placed in on or with women. So, let's first look at the gratitude of it.

We need to be thankful to have both genders present on the planet because that's how we biologically make more people at least up till now. I'm sure at some point we'll have some science where we might need parts of things from both people, but we may not need the whole person. I mean, things examples like artificial insemination and things biological we haven't advanced past . You remove the biological fluid or data that we need and then we have made people. But right now, on this planet, the way the dimension still looks, you need some form of biology to make little humans. Not little souls, because I believe when we come here, we are Soul and the soul that is your child could be older than you are. But I'm talking about babies being born through intimate sexual activity or whatever infertility treatments are needed to get little people here.

They knew that I would experience life differently than they had chosen to experience life because the first feminists I met, were only two camps. It was my mom and all her friends, which I call my Amazon Aunties and I used to call all my blood aunties, my Stepford wife aunties, not in a disrespect for the movie, but in gratitude to them, for all the systems they/ my grandmother and aunts taught me in order to run a house, take care of my husband, take care of my kids. So,it made me the perfect wife and that's how I see the Stepford wives. They are the perfect wife. So, men in our family, don't come home to women with sweats on and a ponytail on top of their head. Now my aunts, my mother, my sisters' don't do things that. They might wear that as some thing very casual as part of their day. Most of them didn't, right and most of them are gone, but you didn't look that way when your husband came home. Maybe you looked like that for laundry, but usually, you didn't even look like that then.

So, I call them that. And then one day they were like, Mia, what if people think we're unhappy in our marriages and(in reference to one of my Masterminds) that's why you said, Stepford wives. I was sad and explained, okay, so I'll change it. So, I changed it to mermaid island where women are rare and beautiful. Mermaids are rare. And so, I was happy with that, okay, but they're beautiful everywhere in museums and they're beloved and fairytales and paintings and operas and ballets and right. All ages of people love them. So, I was very sure, that would be perfect for my aunts because I didn't know how to explain to the world perfect 1950s Housewives with perfect 1940s power. That's who they are. And that's who I am. That's how we were raised. So, you're powerful as a woman and you should powerful enough to love care, and adore and take care of your husband while raising your kids and working if you want to.

So, they're kind of bad butt, but in all aspects, except for the one, the Mastermind exclusive only to my store. That's why you had to be grateful for everyone with the, dreaded you don't get married to get divorced rule meant if you had a husband doing something horrific, you still stayed married. So, my feminist aunties taught me do not take crap off of meat sacks meaning there are tons of men on the planet. There are tons of men that are handsome. There are tons of men with a big one. That's what Richard used to call it. He'd be like big one. So, I prefer to say that and be lady-like, because I'm not so big on cursing or that sort of thing. I tend to just stick with my vernacular and my syntax, but I'll use his, and say big one. They taught us, you know, tons of men have millions of dollars. Tons of men have billions of dollars. Tons of men are super handsome, super cute, super charming. They've got big ones. They've got little ones. There's no thing in this world that you can't do, that you can't have, that you can't be with the exception of you don't have that one body part. Then they would teach me stuff both true and historical, but men can't have kids. So, if the planet was ending... Now realize they were extreme man-hating feminists.

So, they literally would teach me stuff both true and odd this: If the planet were ending and we had to choose, we could repopulate the planet as long as we say the women, because men via donation, there could be corporate building factories, just full of sperm banks. Then we could have sons and make the planet again. But if every woman on the planet died, the human race would die out. Now they didn't say that to me to say, men are useless. We can just milk them like cows and save it and not have to put up with their crap. They said it to say this, women are valuable, women are irreplaceable, and most women don't get that programming. So, although they tried to also give me all the crappy mean hate men, the world that kind of thing. I didn't keep that programming. I saw it, but I didn't take it but the strength and the value, I am not friends with a lot of women. I mean close hangout friends, because for, I don't know, 30 years, I guess my population has been helping women and stopping men who are villains and helping men be happy and healthy and loved. So, women used to complain that I helped men at all. The male population that I helped was 30% of my practice. Then innocent men would complain at 100% of the villains that I worked to stop, and I was like, isn't that how you guys topped out on the percentage of villains. They were asking about bad women, but Mia what about... I was telling them you know we don't hunt villains, More reasons people were unhappy with the world, reply okay and I'd work on that and I'd work on that. I'd work on that, but it was because I didn't have shared programming with women. My companies are known for solving 11 problems in the world.

I was not taught if you like a man and another woman likes a man attack that woman, it was drilled in my head that if your boyfriend or your husband cheats on you, I was taught don't you go after the woman, I literally was taught you go after him. He made you the promise. He's the one that's being disloyal. He's being a dog. He's being a playboy. There's a difference between playboys and dogs and wolves. A wolf and a playboy will get you to agree to his cheating, for whatever reasons. I know men that women agree to keep the money. I know women because they don't want to lose their security. I know women who do it because as long as he's doing that, they don't have to sleep with them, and they hate him anyway because they're gold diggers and didn't want to sleep with them in the first place. So, they don't care who he sleeps with. As long as they get to benefit from his material or wealth, his material attributes, or his power in the world, in a company, or politically. Later in these last 11 years, I've met women who do it out of spiritual power. Let them sleep with whoever he wants to out of the spiritual power they get from him. So, I was raised to don't do that. You don't sell yourself. You don't sell yourself for any reason, which includes marriage. Never accept a cheater, it is spiritually bad for your health.

So, a lot of times I would just be quiet because women were talking about things that I thought were completely unnecessary because I was totally just like a dude mentally, in a pencil skirt and stilettos, or a dude dressed like a doll because I wasn't really a dude, never would want to be one -. I'm one of the girliest girls on the planet until people start to bore me intensely with their cruelty. A lot of women are taught if you like a guy and another girl likes a guy and the guy doesn't like either of you or the guy likes one of you or the other. The guy's not even in their brain. All they can focus on is they need a man. They want a house. They want cars and in order to get that stuff, they need to get it through a man. Men might sell that stuff, but there's this thing where you can make money, and then you could buy that stuff all by yourself. So, the first Mercedes I bought with cash that I saved up and I was 21, 22. At 24, I had that car. So, when women were insecure telling me, oh, you're stupid. I can't believe it. I revealed, I have refused; I have turned down more than you will ever be offered so I'm not like you, I don't fit in with you and your peer pressure, little clickety-click way to call women names or try to strip them of power or bully them so they fit in with the pod. You're not a dolphin, you're a pod of something else.

Something I don't want to be a part of because it includes gossiping as soon as one of your friends leaves the room or being cruel or mistreating your husband or betraying him or lying or cheating or stealing or kissing somebody you don't love. So I wrote a New Mastermind System.

So, there are all these rationalizations, and they all went back to the different ways they hate men. Men did this we have to do this. Heads up one of our classes where we have called the Harpy List and What's your Burger? It's six of our classes, four are put together as a conference and they get one-day training, three-day training, five-day training, or seven-day training with certification. People would say, well, what's the difference between one and three days? I was assuring them time. Time is the difference. The class is the same but how in-depth, what happens and then what is added, and the reason you're there for the class. So, the one-day class is a totally different experience and outcome than the three-day and the three-day is different than the five-day and the five-day is different than the seven-day and not everybody can do the seven-day because if you didn't get it there's no reason for you to be certified because then you could be hurting people. Going around, pretending something.

So, let's say we had a yoga festival. Yoga certification has different times different types of yoga, but there are many of us where you go to a yoga class and, what the heck? Because it's also why you're there. Who you're there, the vibe that's in their class? There are classes where you go and it's like all snakes and they're plugging into you. They're not plugging into the divine. They're just doing poses, plugging into you, gasping on the way there and talking about how they cheat on their husbands on the way out and sometimes learning from the teacher, how to cheat on her husband and use their money and use the guy and mistreat him. When he starts getting older discard him. I don't need that kind of stuff. So, I tend to say, connect, you are Soul. You came from somewhere. You don't even have to figure it out where is. You could say, what am I not receiving that I am believing incorrectly to make me not understand where I came from. You can say that and that is going to get you so many gifts and so many answers and so much new stuff and so much wealth. Our New Mastermind was created to fix these problems.

Money is wealth, yes but money is energy too. Remember you want your money to be happy. You want to be happy with money. You don't want to just have money and be unhappy. Money can be happy or sad. The physical thing, a coin, a bill, a dollar bill, a $100 bill, $50 bill. Money carries an energy that came from us, which means we are source, an energy we take with us, an energy we put out. So why would you want to be seemingly wealthy because of your bank account and be spiritually bankrupt? So that's why we made Time is Gold class. It's actually Time is Pure Gold because pure adds that level of sensuality, sexuality, passion. Not focused on the act of sex. Let's think about it. Everything's not the act of sex. You could have a passion for painting when you finish, ah, that was good. You can have sex with somebody like a mannequin and unless its the beginning the mannequin is trying to work her way into your life to get to your bank account, ask any multimillionaire. Once the mannequin has a way in meaning: a child, a marriage, a contract, some sex magic, a spell. Whatever it is that made the mannequin hook in and be able to have access to your funds.

Once they have that, they don't need you, and the sex you had with that mannequin when you met them while they were using sex magic to get you, is definitely not the sex you have with that mannequin after they have access to your money because they don't need you. So, there's no passion in that sex it's void and usually, they try to make sure that there's a lot of drugs and alcohol involved so you don't realize how empty it is to have sex with a demon that looks like a trophy wife but is a mannequin.

That's what happens when we forget about gratitude and realize wealth is everything that makes us happy. How do we get the wealth of joy, the wealth of happiness, and the wealth of millions and billions? Energy. So, gratitude is the energy that knocks down buildings. Gratitude is the energy that will stop a tsunami. Gratitudes are the energy that makes an unstoppable tsunami. I love being called Mia. Just Mia.

Alignment with source translates into your guidance via connection. Source Energy When you ask it is given. Get good at alignment. I had never asked for anything for me, I only asked my whole life to make the world better.

So, when little kids are being bullied, they will come to me and be like Dr. Morgan... So little kids usually call me Dr. Morgan or they call me Miss Dr. Morgan White because they don't know titles to take out and use one in place of other titles. I have two last names with no hyphen. Maybe on my radio show, people would call me Dr. Mia. Once again the universe gives you what you resist, I used to always be I'm never going to be a first name doctor ie. Dr. Mia. Of course, as soon as you tell the universe that it presents lots of ways for you to have to learn as soul, suck it up. Don't judge.Grow. Be flexible.

So of course, I was Dr. Mia for a long, long time, but little kids getting bullied because there are eight-year-olds on Facebook Live committing suicide because their friends bullied them. And they're the bullies are also classmates. So, they will literally put in comments or send them texts. Yeah. Do it, do it. Nobody loves you. You should go. That's the world that some people are living and experiencing. So, what if you use this power of gratitude and just be peace, thank you. Thank you that I can hear. If somebody is bullying you, so you can really clown them because I clown bullies, like nothing else because they're spiritual bullies. They're energetic bullies.

All bullying is energy. Friend Circles try to force an entire lifestyle.

My sorority sisters were programmed, Women in my sorority have tried to bully me to be like them or not be as shiny and bright. Or they gossip to steal the blessings God sent me because they were envious, but they're Christain. Three of them even stole money from me. Because they're not as shiny and bright or because they, well, don't date men like that, only date men like this. One time we were at luncheon and some of my sorority sisters actually said, "do not date a white man. We are made to be the wives of black men and rich black men do not date poor black men". My reply was you don't get a vote.

I was just looking at them like, I'm so glad I wasn't raised to be weak-minded. I was raised like my sorority founders. I'm so glad I was raised by feminists and Baptist princesses because they taught me God picks and the feminists taught me, don't listen to you. Listen to me. Be strong, help other women. So, God gets the vote, and he gets the veto. Anything I think that didn't get an okay from God big old veto. I don't do it. Why would I listen to you? Because I don't want to be like you. You don't even love your husband. He's fat and bald. Now I have an ex-boyfriend who's fat and bald and I loved him. I adored him. I thought he was so cute, just like a polar bear stood up. I loved and adored him, and he was fat and bald,and I was like, honey, you're adorable to me and I've also dated models and surfer boys, not young ones, old ones when they have some sense and they run a business, but they still have the surfer body. So that's how you get a guy that's technically a senior citizen that has a body of a 30-year-old because he was a surfer, or he works out. So, I'm not saying that you pick somebody based on how they look. I am saying you pick somebody based on how they look to you, not to your social pod/friend circle, and that your social pod that's doing that.

I used to have this phrase until I started growing up because I didn't want to manifest dying more meaning "just my age number growing up". Just because I'm pretty much how I was when I was seven or eight years old. Very Alice in Wonderland, will put my hands behind my back and hold them like a little girl and look up to somebody and ask them my little curious questions in my little dress with a corset or without a corset, but petticoats. I'm very much still me.

My WORK HAS SAVED LIVES FOR 20 YEARS

So, I'm usually in stilettos or over the years, I've become more in my Mary Jane's. It used to be stilettos or Mary Jane's, but now it's very few stilettos, mostly Mary Jane's, mostly Stacy Adams, and then lots of historical high heels, which I think are sexier and cuter than stilettos. But let me get back to these pods of mannequin that have been trying to control women and training women to hurt men. So, these women decided since they feel disempowered, they were going to gossip and men who liked me that they wanted like them, some women even do black magic to women out of envy to hurt innocent women. Real life circumstance a woman is better than you so instead of becoming a better you, they would attack that woman with black magic.

A lot of times, most of the time, it wouldn't be even women they met. Just a woman walking down the street whose dress was prettier. A woman who was smarter or kinder or all the boys like her, none of the boys like you so they attack the women. to cast some spell. I did therapy for tons of witches over the years not because witches helped stop phedophiles whose victims had mental problems, but because I do therapy for women who have been harmed by men harmed by men and/or life and a lot of them were had/become witches and so I don't judge people. So, it's , okay, that's just a fact, that's a numbers fact. Stop judging people.

So, you could have gone and had them maybe make you prettier or something. I don't know. I don't know how to fix that for you. But I do know as a female, as a bio girl, as my friends call me because I have a lot of transgender friends and that's been since I was 13 years old. All around the world and fought for rights or actually donated my art to fight for the right to surgeries, to stop hate crimes against women, things like that. So, they would say, you know, I'm a bio girl, but I'm tall. I'm tall for a woman. I'm always grateful. So, you've got to be grateful for your height. So as a little kid, I was in fifth and sixth grade, I was not the tallest girl in my class because you know how God always hooks you up until you can catch up. So, I wasn't the tallest girl. The tallest girl's dad was six-foot, something, 6' 5 or something. My dad was 6' 1 and my mom was 5' 9 so I was about 5' 6 or 5' 7 in the sixth grade. So, I was as tall as the teacher, but at least I wasn't tall as the tallest girl in the school.

I still wasn't comfortable, and my mom would take me shopping for shoes and stuff and I'd say, why is my size sold out? It's because my feet are too big. She was supportive , no Mia it's because somebody is buying your shoes. So, it was like I always had a subconscious change me back to gratitude. So, I became me, I am grateful that I am taller than most women and shorter than most men. So, I remember sometimes when I meet men, sometimes I forget that some men are uncomfortable about their height, even though I think they're tall. So, I met one and he was like 6'1 and when he picked me up at the airport, I did the little comparison because to me, I wish he had to ask me because I was like hmmm, this guy's really sexy and cute and gorgeous. So, of course, you know, I'm not assuming any insecurities and I don't have any insecurities. Any insecurities I had, I worked on and got rid of them as if they were evil villains trying to invade my space. So, we're now in the house.

So. in our other chapter, we were in one house, the house looks the same, but now we know how to treat it differently by using gratitude to switch it. Look at the world differently by using gratitude. So, I would say I'm taller than most women, but I'm shorter than most men. Then if a man was my height to 6'1 or 6' 2, 6'1 was the top. I would say, that's the perfect height for kissing. Then I literally have exes. Now, I don't have tons of exes because I'm very picky because of the way I was raised, my programming just doesn't accept whomsoever asked me out because you have to get God's approval then you have to get my subconscious expectations of how you get to treat me or not treat me then the not selling my soul, mind, body, I'm not for sale rent or lease. One of my ex-boyfriends I literally can just start the sentence and say, I'm not and he will look up from whatever he's doing or walk over to me and say for sale, rent, or lease because he was used to buying women and people.

So, he just knew, no matter what he did, I loved him, and I wanted to be with him. But if he did anything, like send me a big gift monetary stuff like that. We were really young and so sometimes I would push it until my friend Max told me in my thirties that men need a place in your life and so let him do it right. Let them do that. Let them give what they want to give you as opposed to send the gift back like I used to always do. So, I stopped doing that in my thirties thanks to Maximillian. So, thanks, Maxi. Another gratitude. Now Max was a man who I would call used and abused women because women would do whatever Max wanted to. So, Max would think of torturous things to do with their permission, and they would say they liked it so that they could be with Max. But he never did that to women who didn't let him do it. He never did things

to women without their permission. He liked to do things to women with their permission. So, I was just laughing, Max, I don't believe how you find these women. He would just crack up. I didn't make these women and they're happy. He's like, no, they're always happy. I make sure they're happy. I was like, Maxi maybe and it was more, they let you do it. Sometimes they even ask me to. I'm sad, okay, honey. So, we stayed friends for some time, but Max taught me that about guys.

That's one thing about knowing men who are playboys and men who are the top in their field or running their companies or that sort of thing is they will teach you things about men and how they interact with certain types of women versus other types of women. Then they have this thing about leagues. Is that women in their league or out of that league. So, unfortunately for these women going around doing all this negative energy towards women they envy. Men, their concept of leagues means they always want the woman is out of their league. So, if you're in their league, that's the main problem right there. You see and the fact that leagues exist and the fact that you're trained to hunt them. So, I say, and this is one of our little sayings. Don't try to take it. Don't steal intellectual property. I have taught women two things. If you wouldn't sleep with him if you had a billion dollars, do not sleep with him if he has a million dollars.

Greater is do not hunt men, or you will find beasts. You focus on you and you and what you want and your love and your light and your goodness. Then you'll look up and there will be this dude that you love and adore. Now you can give him your attention and him your energy. But when you wake up in the morning, it shouldn't be to find a man. When you go anywhere, traveling events, dinner, nightclubs, parties it should never be hunting men. It shouldn't even be looking for men. Men are biologically programmed to look for women by the way. As a doctor who specializes in the brain, especially master of the subconscious you need to understand they are biologically programmed to hunt and chase women. The only men who won't do that are men and who have been hurt so bad by mean girls, demons, mannequins that now they don't trust anything with a vagina.

Maybe I shouldn't say vagina because I didn't say penis. But now since I said penis now maybe. Yeah. It's okay. The hipsters don't get me started on you. I've been writing a joke book because you wear me out. I didn't curse for 28 years until God created hipsters. Then I thought, what the? I still said what the? like this little boy. I used to have a little client. He's a little boy. He was so cute. Apparently, his parents cursed a lot to the point where he didn't know cursing was something you weren't supposed to do until they started spanking him for cursing. Then he got confused because he learned it from them and then it was because he was getting older enough to interact with the world and he was cursing but he thought cursing was the language. So, he adapted. This is so you understand how the subconscious works, how gratitude works, how envy works. Instead of being mad at his parents, like, why are you spanking me when I'm just doing what you taught me? He just would stop right before the curse word. So, every curse phrase that he had learned, he just wouldn't say the curse word part.

So, he would be telling a story about something happening at school, something that happened in class. Something happened with these uncredentialed teachers in the classroom, calling themselves teachers and giving the kids A's and B's and the kids don't do work. They just text and play video games and the school policy is everybody gets an A or a B. So, then the parents don't complain. The kids aren't going to tell that they're not having to do work, but it shows up in the fact that when they graduate, they have no education. So, he was telling me, you know, one of those kinds of stories that I've heard a lot over 25 years, I guess, 28 years. Yeah, 28 years. He was constantly going, what the... What the... What the... But he would not say the F-bomb. He wouldn't say the rest of the word because he had been spanked so many times by his constantly cursing parents that their sentences, most sentences that came out of their mouth were composed of curse words. So, he took the curse words out of the sentences and still use the sentences. So, it was hilarious.

When little kids come for bullying, I teach them tsunami meaning they have to become a force of gratitude to the point where you literally look at somebody and I usually tell them you don't get a vote. So, imagine there's somebody in your face, spewing crap. When you do that to me, what I usually do based on my spiritual gifts is whatever's in you or on you starts to show itself. So, I start to see you looking like a crocodile or whatever it is, your negativity. I just see you turning into black smoke or tar. I'll just see you, see the real you and while you're doing that, I'm totally just thinking of all the stuff I'm grateful for in the world, wash you out, stay at zero. Be like the famous Hawaiian doctor be like kahuna. Yeah. Stay at zero. So, I just let you do your little stuff and I'm not afraid of anything, blah, blah, blah, blah, blah. Then right when you're done, I specialize in the brain. So, I just go, you don't get a vote, and usually, they're quite stirred because energetically, they didn't get inside me. Energetically there's no fear. There's no anger. There's no envy. There's no doubt. I didn't lower my vibe. I increased my vibe. Then I say, you don't get a vote and that messes with their head because their subconscious is like, oh, wow. Yeah. Okay. They usually get confused and walk away or they might be more monsters and then you've just got to be like (whoosh) tsunami. I said, no. I said, no.

So, mannequins are scary because there are demons that have enough plastic surgery or fakeness to appear to be women. You can dress a mannequin. When you buy a mannequin, it can be at Bergdorf's. It can be at Walmart. It can be at a children's or it can be anywhere. Mannequins are everywhere but based on the clothes, you put on them that same mannequin looks like it fits in that place. That's why you put them in store windows, but they are still a mannequin. There's still a hollow. There's still a demonic thing with a vagina that they're prepared to use. So, if you buy a mannequin and you didn't know, you bought a mannequin by the time you found out... That's why we started that class because there were too many, there were hundreds. See, I think one is too many, but there were hundreds and over the year showing me to be thousands, tens of thousands of men who were being captured, kidnapped, and tortured by mannequins because they're afraid to lose their millions. If they leave her or they leave one and they think, oh, it's that person and then they find another mannequin.

Mannequin comes in all shapes and styles. Google to wear a mannequin and you're going to find when you have a store, you can get a silver mannequin. I've had leather mannequins before, but they're hollow. All of them are hollow on the inside. Some mannequins are completely dumb just like the ones in his store that come with no head. Some mannequins are enhanced. We never used to have that. All mannequins had an average size booby, but now thanks to plastic surgery, you can get big ones on a mannequin. You can plasticize the mannequin more, but she's not a doll. Dolls are women who are beautiful and kind and loving and smart and full of positive energy, who might tell you that your crappy behavior men are not okay. So usually, you get kidnapped by a mannequin because the doll you wanted said, but I don't want you to cheat on me or the doll you wanted said, please don't yell at me, or the doll you wanted said, I want to work. You're a billionaire with a wife who wants to work. You're like, no, I want somebody who doesn't work so that all of your time can be spent on me.

One of my exes told me, I don't want you to have children because what if I want you to go somewhere and you can't go because there was a child. I was like, wow, you have thought out your selfishness into the future. Wow, that could be a movie. That could be a movie like how this book and this movie, and this talk and my classes take you through different types of time and space and consciousness and realities. Do you know what it takes for a person to figure out that their girlfriend that they love should not have children because one day in the future they might want to go somewhere, and they won't be able to go because there's no babysitter? People grow and people change, and people get different levels of maturity and consciousness. You can have a 60-year-old and a 70-year-old that still has the mentality of a 20-year-old.

That can happen but usually, we learn, we grow, we go, oh, that was a mistake or that wasn't love. They may not even go to what that was, but they'll know that it wasn't love. So, you just thank them, thank you for being in my life. I still love you even though you said that I know that if I have a baby, you'll still love the baby and me because you have a great heart and you love me, but that little part that's selfish thank you for showing it to me. So, you can always just say, thank you. Thank you. Thank you. Don't say thank you for hitting me unless you say thank you for hitting me early, so I know to leave you now instead of waste years of my life. Notice how thank you is still part of that sentence. Thank you for showing me who you are.

By the way, I only have eight exes and one ex-husband so that's nine. I'm picky, so, okay. God has to approve so they got God's Approval. It's very strange when you think that one of them is hilarious. They're all hilarious to me. There's one that's so serious, he's always serious like verging on grumpy but the rest of them are funny, like funny, and crack jokes. Say funny stuff to make me laugh or say funny stuff that makes me laugh. But when it comes down to it, if you think of how people want to relate, what they tend to do is you can always tell if someone loves you. If they're figuring out how to make you a part of their life and they forget the parts of you so that you still have a life. That's not a trick question. That's a reframe.

When two people get together, they become parts of one another's lives is what we think. But in truth, when two people come together, they make a life. That's why two become three. One plus one is three, because that three, that third thing is the energy created by those two people. You can take that same man, put them with a different woman or same-sex, put them with a different person and you're going to get that third thing is going to be different. The energy created by two people in a relationship. The relationship is the third thing. That differs, which means you can be in a relationship with a guy and he's a totally different man in a different relationship with another woman. Now, I believe energetically that happens for a lot of reasons, but one of the main reasons is you weren't supposed to be with him. So, a toxic relationship has to do with those two people. Those two people are toxic together, but one of them usually not both, one of them with another person, different .

The perfect way in this house that we're in of gratitude and thankfulness. Beauty tames the beast. Red tames the wolf. Women who are dolls have the ability for monsters to love them and not be monstrous. Mannequins have the ability to make good men, bad men or pollute them until they become like monsters and demons. They also have the ability to hook up with a man who is a monster or a demon, and then let them cheat so they can go suck the light out of other women. The man nor the woman in that relationship has a light or goodness. So, in order to have luck and goodness and joy, they go and have affairs with other people so they can suck up your light and suck up your joy or get healing from their own darkness. So, if you buy a mannequin, the mannequin may not care who you sleep with because the mannequin wants you polluted and the mannequin is feeding off of your soul, and every time you encounter something good, they feed off of you like caviar. That's why you have to watch.

If you've got millions of dollars or you're very successful in your career and you love it and you have a mannequin and you can't figure out why you're unhappy, check around your house and see if you bought a mannequin you didn't know. Check around your house and see if there's any joy, see if there's any health and healing. As a matter of fact, if you're in your house right now, walk outside your house and walk back in and see if it feels cold. Do you live in a mausoleum because you bought a mannequin, and you don't know you bought a mannequin? Those are the ways you tell and because there are women training women to become mannequins. So now you've got the average woman thinking chase men, hope one of the boys likes them. That kind of thing,

These women, the mannequins who are offering classes and stuff will find these women and say stuff like come to my class and we will pretend like we're selling this and we'll pretend like we're doing this and they're training them how to use magic and energy, stuff they put in your food, the energy they send to make you buy the mannequin. So, they are , I call them mannequin factories. Now it's not like they're advertising with the exception of the one who teaches them about going to places, going to these camps and they teach you little tricks of how to plant yourself, where there are rich men and pretend to be rich so that the rich man gets disarmed because you're not after his money because you have more money than him, but really you don't.

I give most of my money away to charity. I always have, and I work for free for charities. Then I'm really expensive per person. When I say expensive, I actually think I'm not expensive because that's what my clients told me. My clients told me to raise my rates because I was too cheap because of the value that they get. Their problems get fixed permanently forever for this and every lifetime. So, they're like, do you know how much money I spent trying to fix that problem? What you charged me even after I increased my price like they told me that was less than 1% of what I fixed to have lived with this problem for 20 years. You fixed it and three to five sessions or 10 hours, that kind of thing. Four hours, five hours, you fixed it and it's gone. I was like, yeah and it's not coming back.

So, I was at conferences in fields where I work to make the world a better place and I started being around men who had millions, who weren't happy-go-lucky playboys that I saw at events. They were not alpha males. Some of them were trapped by mannequins, most of them are trapped by circumstance. So, the circumstance is the same condition living in the mausoleum, all that but their wife's not evil. Their wife was just a woman that they thought was safe and they didn't feel as attracted to her. They married her because she was safe. Some men safe means she's average looking enough to not cheat on me or the men will say, I feel that I'm average looking and so I'll marry a wife that matches that, and then that'll help grow my career because I can't get a beautiful woman. Then later when they get more money than they're buying gold diggers and mannequins and trying to entice maybe 18-to-20-year-olds from impoverished nations or from impoverished circumstances where they're like , okay, I'll date a 70-year-old man because he'll give me money and so they'll go and do that, and they'll get paid for it. But what the old men haven't realized is these camps and types of mannequins that have been producing these women not to be what they were initially historically.

Initially and historically these women were more docile, and they fawned on the man and they loved him, and they saw him kind of like a savior. You saved them from poverty, so they always have loyalty. Then the men started showing disrespect, cheating on them and stuff, or thinking they're above them, that kind of thing. So, when the dynamic energetically changes from, look I've got an 18-year-old and I'm 70 and she's treating me like she's out. What they didn't see is there have been clients now and friends who are like, I'm sick in the hospital Mia and I think it's this girl that I just flew from Russia. I'm like, what? They say, you told me to listen to my soul and my soul says, it's her but I flew her here because she's young enough not to cause problems. Sometimes men think women over 35, especially women in their forties have been so mistreated by previous men that men think it's harder to date them because they're jaded towards the world men will hurt me.

But if they date women too young to know the pains and atrocities accumulated in their space from bad relationships, that they're naïve enough that they can manipulate these girls and use them for sex. They're satisfied with you bought them a house or a diamond or a yacht, whatever it is for your social class. But their goal is to have women who won't cause them trouble. What they're getting is mannequins who are there for their soul, their money sometimes they try to kill them with actual poison or energetic poison messing with their food. Literally, the guy, that particular guy, and this has been about 2,700 dudes. One guy had the same pattern as 19 dudes. He flew someone here. They were a certain age. He flew to where they lived, met them, picked from amongst the girls because the girls were raised an American will come and give it.

So, sell yourself because that's the best life you can have, or that's the best way to have a prosperous life that kind of thing. But they were also taught, these are bad men because they are buying little girls, so you don't have to treat them nice, and you don't have to respect them, and you don't. They're just waiting because he's older. So, they're waiting for him to die. Well, that dynamic changed about 10, 16 years ago, but it became very prevalent about 10 years ago where, yeah, they're like a sleeper cell. So, now you've got a sleeper cell mannequin. You've got a five-year-old raised to be a mannequin, knowing that she waits. She waits. She waits. She waits. She waits until you're old enough. She's been there long enough and then she turns the tables. If you leave, I'm taking more than half or I'm taking all of it and you're going to be old, feeble, sick sitting in that chair watching me date young men.

So, that's what this one wanted. She actually did spiritual work, energetic attacks, black magic, and poisoned his food and he was hospitalized. I hadn't seen that before. I didn't know that was a thing. I knew someone that was experiencing that as a thing, but those people were attacking me so that's why I was able to see specifics, oh, somebody is doing this. The guy who called me was already in the hospital and he just wanted to know Mia, why am I in the hospital? Why I'm in the hospital and why does my soul keep telling me it's her? He could have been in the hospital because he's old. He could have been in the hospital because he has been a wild partier, rock, and roller that has done whatever he wanted for 60 years, 55, 60 years, and now he's late 70s, early 80s. Another one just turned 70 and they did what they wanted to. So, they knew when they die, they're probably not going to die with a wife because they wanted a whole bunch of girlfriends or they wanted five or six girlfriends or one. If they're hippies, they call them wifelets. They've had 20- or 30-year relationships with six to nine women and all the women know about each other.

This was a new game that nobody told men about the production of mannequins. So, you better stay in a house of gratitude. You better stay with the thank you because that's enough to feed you if a mannequin is draining you. That's enough to give you hope so that when the mannequins are pushing telepathic energy into your space you can keep your thoughts clear. So, he was out of the hospital two days after I got the call because we identified the who, what, where, why, how. How to fix the energy and the girl ended up in the hospital and then she left. She had to leave the country. What she planned, what she showed visibly was she wanted him not to die. She wasn't trying to kill him. She wanted him to be incapacitated so that he could be old and feeble, and she could run around and have lovers and he would have to watch that in his house. For her, it was revenge for women, it was revenge for him having come to her country and bought her.

He didn't pay for her but come to her country where she was raised that she had no other choice than to pick the men with the highest bank account that likes her and then live with him and do whatever he says. Marry him, have kids, that kind of thing. Like I said, some guys are doing that just so they don't have trouble with women. They're not doing it. They're not pedophiles, they're not buying 12-year-olds. These girls are 18 to 22, usually no more than 21 because the guys got a little greedy and naïve in what was happening. But these women were raised to pretend to be the docile little creatures based on age and country, 9 different countries and men of wealth know where to go, which countries they are, and if you want, I can give you the list. In choosing these women, they chose their downfall and these young women had planned from the time they were little kids to do this in 20 years. Our Classes because I've now had enough clients to know how to fix it. OUR Mastermind. GOLDEN ARIGATO

ALICE: BE RARE IN ANY WORLD ESPECIALLY IN RABBIT HOLES

Now, keep in mind, many men who went to these struggling countries to get wives just thought they couldn't get wives in a normal way. They wanted wives. They didn't want girls just to have relationships with. Women who are villains , These camps where women are traveling to countries and teaching them how to trick, American men and then marry them, use them, then leave the men when they're older, when the girls are 35 to 40. They are teaching them a plan to harm nice men later. These are not men who wanted anything but love and a family. Then there are camps and classes where women trick rich alpha males by 50-200 women rotate sharing a membership or suite in a hotel from an app to appear to have money.

It was like falling into another Rabbit Hole when I found out this level of cruelty towards men was happening. Nice men being tricked by demonic women in Hawaii and the men thought this would be the way that they could have a beautiful or a cute wife without themselves being alpha males. These are women not what they expect. They expect a wife, not expect to be left when they're old and it all to have been a trick. a sleeper cell.

A woman is training women to hurt men. When I met a woman Li Yin Anderson she claimed she was selling Young Living Oil but later she tried to recruit me to use my degrees and skills to do trainings at mansions with her. Everywhere she went I witnessed her gas lighting. She was going around the world training women to trick, deceive, and hurting men. She tried to deceive me to writing her training to get the women who were seeking spiritual growth take their market women to do this harm men with long term plans. She was not spiritually connected to God. Her goal was to trick all the people around her. I was tricked and shocked got away from her soon as possible, oh my goodness, what the girls are seeing spiritually somebody is doing this on purpose in the physical world. These are not individual girls that are coming up with these ideas. These are not mean girls that went bad. They while allegedly teaching women on the Asian continent how to sell Young Living Oils. LiYin, Li Yin she spells her name different ways even LeeYin had orchestrated a way to cheat on her husband around the world and train women to be evil hollow souls using negative energy and manipulations they were producing what my company calls mannequins and I didn't know women like this existed; this was something. I met her at Yoga Festival. Now, sometimes the universe tries to send me/you things that you didn't know happened in the world so that you know what's happening in the world. But other times as we enter into the third house, we'll call it the I love you house. I like to call it mi amor. It's to help us stop something in our future. Expose it to make the world better.

A living lie. Polluted love stories I had heard these all over the world usually from females of the species bragging about their actions, to destroy males while pretending to love their husbands or boyfriends.

Vibrational Reality my Mom was a Feminist so I don't take part in mean girl games or gossip so when women approach me to try to tick me into accept a fake friendship I don't even know the girl games they play because it was never a part of my encoding my programming.

I'm built completely different. That's why I'm much more like ALICE and hang out with friends who are wild rich men who are always gentlemen big brothers, fans and wolves or gay besties.

Not like VIBE meowMia like MiaMeow, not the cosplay type of thing. A funny joke class about mean girls My class for couples about true love. I mean, literally love the house of love where you adore that person and you call them little names that just come out of you, that you can't help. If you're like me, I'm kind of like a cold fish sometimes because I'm a quirky, funny, genius who was raised to be a feminist so I try to kept my silly wild self under control when I am doing business to be serious. So, I'm gushy and mushy when I'm your girlfriend (like your personal geisha) but I'm always good. I always look out for treatment towards little kids and old people. BUUT...when I'm not your girlfriend. meaning if a guy comes towards me and goes, you are so beautiful. I'm not going to blush and gush and laugh and go, oh, thank you so much. I'm going to say, thank you very much. I appreciate that. "You're wonderful" like an innocent child and end with "I appreciate the compliment".

So, I love you, how you would say it to God is how you should say it to somebody you're willing to marry. Not that I think you should love anybody above God. But I do think the feeling that you have, where you say, I love you. So, if you just said, I love you 108 times. I love you. I love you. I love you. I love you. I love you. I love you. I love you. It changes the vibe. It changes the vibe in your body. It changes the energy around you. It changes the energy of the person you're saying it to. Now imagine you don't feel like anybody loves you and someone says that. They must be lying unless you come up with tests for them to constantly prove it. And this causes problems in relationships. But that is basic human relationships. Not this demonic crap I learned about in Hawaii women coming from other places training and manufacturing mannequins to be plotting gold digging demons not satisfied to capture a KOI but to hold and ultimately destroy the KOI.

I specialize in the Brain

FULL BRAIN CAPACITY ENERGETIC WAVE PATTERNS and I am a the subconscious, cleaning, healing and reprogramming it. Cinderella

So, imagine there was a game, men knew if you wanted a good wife, that wasn't going to be gold-digging or a liar or a cheater who would do whatever you say and love you and think you're their hero from saving them from poverty and bringing them to America.

These men took part in a very old game that maybe should never have existed on the planet. If we want to get into the coulda woulda shouldas maybe, we should never have set up a system where women told their daughters sell yourself, that's the best, you've got going for you because you're a girl. Maybe we should never have done that but then they probably were taught that by women who were suffering and were like, woo, I wish an American would come buy me. But this started in CaveMan times. Well now nobody told men that's not love because you're not going to be loved.

Remember we're in the house of amor, the je t'aime Vibe. The reason that class was called Mia meow because it's a child there were these two characters and all they said to each other was meow meow and not everybody understood them but they always understood each other. That's the mode we should be in now je t'aime. They're in a house where they think they're loved and a 20-year-old and an 18-year-old usually see the world differently because the more we give permission to people and when I say permission, any a-hole any evil person, any abuser, anybody who hurts you. I'm not saying you gave them permission to do it. What I'm saying is don't let them steal your joy because they did it. Don't let them win.

So now you don't even realize when you're 30 that you don't have as much joy and as much sparkle and as much goodness as you did because you didn't give up or clean out one or the other people. Maybe you thought you gave it up, but there is still a little hate or still some sadness, something still in you, inside your Vibe/Soul.

So, you can be 50 or 60 and have the joy or even more joy than you did when you were 18, as long as you're cleaning like Ihaleakala, he's a famous Hawaiian doctor because you stay at zero. You forgive, you get it out of you. Most people say a woman at 18 is a different woman at 50 because they're counting on her to have the accumulation of heartache and disappointment. So, her vibe is different, her glow is gone. Her sparkle is gone then there are women that are 75 years old, still have their sparkle, still have their joy. It's not because bad stuff didn't happen to her, it's because she or someone like me got it "out of them" and got their sparkle back, their joy back, or even more sparkle and joy and wealth.

So, these men wanted love. What they got was obedience. They could have toughed it out in America and just went with the women in the country they were born in, there are women in every country that would love them and would like them instead of part of the game built for the males and the species where you go to other countries and then there's a wife programmed that women do what you say because you're the husband and women do what you say and you pay the bills, they fix the house, they're grateful.

Now I was raised like that except for the grateful part. When you're only grateful to your husband you don't love him. As a doctor on a subconscious level you're saying to them "I'm grateful for not being where I was" you are not saying "I'm grateful for YOU" you're not saying "I'm grateful for the gift that you are because I love you so much". You're only saying "you're the thing that made me not starve. I have to behave and do what you want so I don't go back to starving sometimes".

ROBBING WOMEN OF ABUNDANT MIND

Men didn't realize that this makes hateful women and it makes men replaceable, accidently vibrationally make women feel that they can replace you with someone else who doesn't make them starve what you finally produced was it breed of women in the last two generations figure it out instead of constantly getting a "new keeper" why not destroy him and have the money, his money instead of replacing him with another man with money when Why wait to become a widow. You have after you trick them at your disposal and will always obey and he can cheat and do whatever he wants as long as he brings the money home. This was the first game was ever played in history not in mass, although no more than two women per century. There are many stories in 1400-2001 massive where very young women were forced to marry a Very Old Man and those young women waited for him to die, a few entered with the goal to make herself a rich Widow. I thought these were the stories of horror stories monster selectly taken over the young women's bodies from the trauma that was locked into the body. Not a new game in town.

Lavender Fields

I was raised to take care of my husband. I was raised to take care of my house. I was raised to take care of my children and I do it so well that I had a DIY Television show, years ago just showing all my little systems. I teach and taught classes to raise money for charities, to fund stopping pedophiles. I adore my husband and show him by using those skills and systems. So, I am so good at it, it doesn't even phase me.

I could have six kids, nine kids, and a husband, and a huge house and my companies and his companies, and I wouldn't even bat an eye never stress about it. It would be easy for me to take care and juggle all of that and have everybody be happy including me, especially me. It is my family coding. But there are some women who can't do that. They can't even take care of two children well, or they take care of the children well, but their house is a mess, or they take care of the house, but the children are awful or ill-behaved or ill-mannered or uneducated. I taught parenting classes for years. Husbands are uncared for. Or women that do all the mundane well but stop having sex with their husband. In my family, our husbands don't even have to buy new underwear. Firstly, Men are whole humans. They're not infants that need to be taken care of every moment. Most men's egos like to be taken care of every moment or be cared for.

So, in the house of love, understands the difference between passive aggressive cared for, cared about, and taken care of. So, men, it's like they're not eight. They want to go buy suits that they want. But when we do our laundry, we are taught as little girls that as we put our husband and our children's laundry away, we're supposed to pull out things that are worn out and buy new ones. So, if our husband's underwear has stains or holes or anything like that, we don't even say anything to them. We replace them; trashing the old or cut them and turn them into rags for outside when he washes the cars and just new things magically appear in their drawer. We want them to feel the love that we have for them in every aspect of their life. Because of social class we don't iron their suits But we know how to. So, we're not raised to think that we are less than but think because we love them their lives should be better.

ARIEL loved the prince. FOR MY NEXT TRICK

In the Spiritual Realm all those people are still attached to you . Everyone you have ever slept with. I am a mixed race person. The best attributes of every one but this did not make for an easy childhood.

I was told I didn't match.
CONSTRUCTED HOSTILE ENVIRONMENT

Now you're going to hear me say, I'm sorry a lot. The women in my family, have no fear about being replaced. We don't even think other women are better than us. No. We have no fear of being replaced or even getting old. The old women in my family they've got young boyfriends, boyfriends their age, but they always have a boyfriend or a husband as men seek them. Men seek us. A vibrational connection to to satisfaction. We don't seek men. We were raised that to never do that. But there is something about our strength, our kindness, our beauty, our spiritual skills. The seventies would say our aura. The eighties would say our wherewithal as women, which that wherewithal by the way was born in the 1940s in America. Because of the

World Wars women got the subconscious permissions to have the wherewithal. So, I'm sorry. I'm not a man. Thank goodness. I don't want to be a man. I love being a woman, but I also love men how they are and if you don't love a man how he is, go and love a different man.

So, the reason they don't have a concept of, oh, they're going to get too old, and then they have to settle for a man they wouldn't love and pretend to love. That's the one thing you don't ever do pretend to love. You love your husband. Husbands deserve to be loved. So, the way we take care of our husbands so that they know they are loved, know that when they walk in the house, they are loved, know that they are adored just based on the emotional satisfaction and feeling they get. When they walk into their own home. When they leave work, they are looking forward to coming home. When they are at work, they're focused on work because they're at peace because they know there is nothing at the house that they have to fix when they get back because any problems that come when your husband's not home, you fix them. If they're too big and you can't figure out how to fix them, then you call your husband during the day and you ask him one or two things, (a team) but there's not a house of drama and trauma and hate and unkindness.

Nope, as you go home, you know, there's nothing, you know, as a man, when you go home, there is no problem. There's most likely cooked dinner. My grandmother ran a company, had six kids, had a three-story house. Everything was always perfect, and I don't mean perfect in the way of like, women are like, I can't handle this. I need to go to therapy. I mean, she had the system that I was taught. So, she just stuck with the systems when to wash your crystal, when to wash your China. Never walked past a washing machine or a dryer without putting something in or taking something out. Things that made doing all that easy and fun and have the satisfaction of it. She was very special. She wasn't like, you should be grateful, and everybody should love me. But when her kids grew up, she did think everybody calls me once a day so that I'll know all my kids are okay and that they cared enough to know how my day was or that I was... So, you didn't have to like talk to her long. She did it based on their personalities.

So, I had one uncle. He'd always be the last one to call and when I would call my grandma, she would give like the list because most of us went by her house every day. So, imagine you've got six kids, you've got grandkids and even though on Sundays, everybody had to go at the same time and be together throughout the day, the other days of the week, you kind of went like before work, after work, after school, on the weekends. So, Saturday was your day where she was just like, well, I'm getting ready for Sunday. Anybody who wants to come by, help or visit while I do this stuff for Sunday. But Monday through Friday as her grandchildren were grown and her children were grown all she wanted was that each of them called her because she missed them. She still ran her companies, and she still took care of her

husband.

Do you know, my grandmother used to drive my grandfather lunch an hour each way across the city in which she lived. I lived three blocks from my grandparents and our house was a big ranch-style house with a white picket fence and roses and it was the length of the city block. So, our houses length was the width of the city block. I didn't have a backyard neighbor because another house or two could have been back there, but they weren't, it was my house. So, my grandparents had a three-story house. That's why we had a ranch-style house because my mother grew up...

I'm sorry, mom, but I'm not running up and downstairs. I spent my childhood doing that. I don't want to do that anymore. So, that's why we had one level. Lots of room, one level because of the way she grew up. So, it was so funny, and I'd say, grandma, you know, people still love you even if they don't call every day. She said, yeah, but they know that I want them to call every day because that shows me, they love me. So, that's an I'm sorry. I'm sorry, but this is what I need. I understand people have childhood can create different love needs.

I'm sorry that I didn't understand the world worked differently, but I need this in my life so I can feel loved. Still looks like the same house, but the house of love has these clarifiers based on who's loving you and who's in it. So, everybody knew they loved her whether or not they called her every day, but she needed that phone call because that's what it meant to her. So, the I'm sorry was, I know that's a little shellfish and she was the baby of nine kids, but she had six kids and she gave them great lives. Do you see what I mean?

People Are Dying From Lack of Hope via an orchestrated manipulation.

So sometimes there's a little something that we do for people because they need it based on something that has nothing to do with us. Just like with God, sometimes we have to go with God. Right. That's why he's the fourth part of the Ho'oponopono. I'm sorry. I'm sorry I didn't know that these types of games are being played on men. I'm sorry I didn't know that women were casting spells to keep rich men kidnapped and kidnapped means they can't figure out how to leave. There is a little bit more than the average millionaire where it's just like, ah, I got $8 billion. I'm going to have to give her $4 billion. What am I doing it for? Then they meet some woman they just love and they're like, you know what? It's worth $4 billion dollars for me to go be happy for the rest of my life. They go and they leave. Well, that's easier than women casting spells and doing stuff to make them stay so they can't leave and go be happy. So, I had to say to God, I'm sorry, Lord. I did not know this was a thing I did not know this was something that existed. But thank you for sending me the two people that showed me this was happening to people.

I'm sorry. I didn't know. I'm sorry I didn't know people would do that to someone they love. I'm sorry that some people were loveless. I'm sorry the mannequins exist. I'm sorry I did not know. You can also say I'm sorry to help me be more. I'm sorry help me love more. I'm sorry help me be better at picking. I'm sorry help me be more light, more loving, more conscious, more giving or you can say, sorry, I don't know the answer. Why don't you tell me, I'm sorry? I don't know the answer. Tell me tonight while I'm sleeping so when I wake up out of the answer, I'm sorry. I don't see this and I'm getting so much worry sent to my brain that I can't spiritually hear myself. So, I'm sorry that I didn't remember what you told me in my dreams. So, send something in the physical world so that I can fix this problem.

So, when we are functioning in the world, somebody might need something. We are not prepared to give because we didn't know that was part of being in a relationship. Like my friend Max women who meet Max don't know that Max does not feel that he's handsome as all the other boys, because he's not as tall as the other boys. This special stuff where women let Max do things that harm them, and they still love him and even will thank him for it and take their allowance. He's not paying women to let him do it. That's boring because then he could just pay women and those women will let him do it. He wants women who like him and love him to do things that they would never do to just do them for him because that will show him that they actually do love him. That's not healthy but it's not to be judged because healthy is relative. We can say that's not healthy because we're like, ooh, what are those two people thinking of? But then did we say, I'm sorry, what are those two people thinking of? What are those two people were experiencing? Is the victim really the victim or the victim of the villain who just got to a point where they met a bigger villain?

So, that's what the mannequins are doing. The mannequin saw themselves historically women were being shipped off to other countries, not trafficking, married. Someone else in another country for the advantage of that country, that translated to their mothers teaching them how to manipulate those men. That then changed for another 30 years. That then changed to this is the only way you're going to do it. So, then resentment is attached and when resentment attaches in love, it's no longer love. I'm sorry you can call it whatever you want but when resentment becomes part of your love language, that is not love. It can be blackmail. It can be energetic harm. You don't have to actually buy stuff, cast a spell and talk to demons to become one. Very often I think a lot of the people at church, become demons and they don't even know it because they think the whites of your eyes have to turn black and you've got to talk in a guttural voice. No. Be unkind, be unloving, be something like a filthy or cold space.

Be something where negativity enjoys being instead of run and from. So, we'll use the Cinderella fairy tale. She actually belongs to house two. Snow. White belongs to house one, but this is Ariel's house, the house where the sea witch makes a deal because she envies. So, she's not trying to help Ariel. When those fairytales were written before or cars and lights and cameras and pavement, phones, electricity.

Before any of that existed, these stories are written to tell us about humans and ways to be. So, when the sea witch tries to get area, that deal, something's just saying you want something you weren't born with instead of appreciating what you have or developing something close to what you want. If you let me use a part of you, hint, hint, I will give you special gifts and special powers and everything you wish for.

Those fairytales tell us, don't make a deal. Don't sell your soul. That's what the fairytales are there for. But when you aren't in the I'm sorry, I didn't see how good I have it. I didn't know people were like this. I didn't know the world was like this. I didn't know the sea witch was going to betray me. I didn't know the sea witch wasn't granting my wishes but making me smaller because she saw my real power, so she wanted to cost me, love. Okay. That's what girls do. There are some girls, not every girl, but there are girls who are the sea witch. I met a girl once. It was so funny because I was with my friends who are biologically different genders than they live as, or they were born biologically different.

So, one girl said Mia you are so as a princess, all guys, even guys who live as women call you princess. You are like the epitome of being a woman, but not girly-girly, but strong like Wonder Woman. You are something that I hate, and I said, what. She said yeah. She said you don't seem to understand why people do stuff for no reason. So, I'm going to tell you the reason. I was, okay, well I was calling the mean girls evil queens, but I know so many queens as in men who dress as gorgeous, beautiful women, or live as gorgeous, beautiful women or become gorgeous, beautiful women that she was just like, okay, so I'm going to say it like this. She's like, I love you. and I hate you. I was like, you hate me all the time. She said, no, I just want to hit you sometimes because, and she said that she has resting B face. She said, no matter what, no matter how girly she wishes, she was, it'll never happen. She'll never be those girls.

So, the evil queens hate the princesses. So, the evil Queens aren't the mannequins, but mannequins can be evil Queens. So, if the mannequins start casting spells to keep men, they don't love that. They just want their money trapped and then the mannequin is a full-on demon and then the evil queen, part of them is casting spells on the women on the man. They don't even care about it. They don't care if that man lives or dies, they just want his money. So, when he wants to leave and be happy, they're willing to kill him to keep the money and they're willing to attack any woman magically, energetically in order to hurt the woman, to make the man not see her, not want her or for the woman not to trust the man. So, she was saying, and imagine we're at a picnic. Imagine a picnic with 25 drag queens and three girls.

One girl is a drag king, which means she dresses as a man in a competition because

in the contest, a literal contest where people won't even think that she's a woman.

So, she's a drag king, the girl I'm talking about, one lesbian and me. So, when you look, the visual is drag queens, a frilly princess, her telling me that sometimes she has to catch herself because she was the kind of girl before she became a lesbian feminist. She was the kind of girl who was the evil queen because she didn't like herself. When you don't like yourself, you encounter people, especially if they share your gender who do like themselves. So, the evil inside of you, the negative energy inside of you attacks them, attacks their energy, attacks that person that is completely innocent and you know why they're attacking because you're innocent and they want you to not to be.

THOUGHTS CAN SHAPE THE ENERGY

So, I want you to spiritually look at the world as a whole bunch of different worlds. Look... at oh God, what was the name of that show? They time traveled. They kept trying to get back to their earth, but they kept encountering worlds that look like their world, multiverses, but each something would be just slightly different. Functionality different. Conscious different. Time traveler, time. I'll have to figure out the name of that.

PANTHEONS COMPARE CROSS REFERENCE CHART

So, as a little kid, I used to watch this other show called Quantum Leap and I thought it was a scientific way to prove how to access past lives because I was born with my spiritual gifts. Then I developed them, and they developed fast and high. The more I changed my consciousness, the more I learned stuff and knew stuff and the things I chose to do with my gifts and the things I never chose to do. That's what gives you more gifts or less gifts. They don't tell you that... Just like we revealed the secret game of the mannequins. When you have spiritual gifts, you can do all kinds of things with them. I usually help find missing children and I help remove things from people's meridians.

Erratic Space Motion: I began studying anatomy in second grade so soon thereafter just the basic physical world was boring to me . Luckily I had my gifts.

SCIENCE & MAGIC the ALCHEMY OF WHAT LOVE IS

Quantum leap was quantum physics. Actually, we'll just say Quantum Leap was about leaping through time. I believe you can leap through time based on consciousness. That's what remote viewing is.

KOI: KING OF INDUSTRY

Women Wicked in their Soul hunt so they can destroy the man energetically in the ole days women cast spells to make a man put them in a position as wife. Now Wicked women never wanted or loved the KOI , KOI are hunted for their wealth. They fly in from other countries or choose older KOI who have been controlling women for years.

Tales of Mermaids and Ariel loved the KOI so much, see she moved past the world she knew and stayed Love.

ROME: I run around Rome as much as possible to say hello to ALL the statues from my favorite childhood stories.

I learned about this world from the PRINCESSES Created by Hans Christian Andersen and my beloved Brothers Grimm. And Princess Pi'ilaniwahine II mother of daughter Queen Lonoma'aikanaka and son Lono of Moana House.

ENERGY IS AN INVISIBLE THING THAT EFFECTS EVERYTHING

SIGHTINGS OF A OF A MANNEQUIN 1ST TYPE EVIL QUEEN ENCOUNTER TYPES

By that time, I'd already agreed to you know, basically give up my stuff and not work on any new projects so that I'd be ready. When he handled everything he was not telling me right. That he needed to handle, but he would tell me parts of the plan and where he was and give me a little timeline in that. So, from the day we met, we came up with ways that we talk to each other. That was a certain vernacular and the manner in which I spoke and he spoke. So, he never was just like "stop being you", can't you speak less formally because I was just me. And I would never say, can you speak less wildly? Because that was just him. And we would talk. And, you know, if I had certain, not just, we didn't just have certain names for each other, we also had certain usage of vocabulary to kind of let the other one know, you are too wild right now, or that is so sexy or you earned those marks. Right. And so, we had this system of constantly not judging and affirming one another.

And then I could tell when its energy wasn't really him. And I would say to him, why did you say blah, or I can't understand why you said this, or if you say that again, and he would say to me, I said that I don't even remember saying that. He said, why would I say that? And I was confused, I don't know. And I have some times where I communicated, where I didn't even remember the communication and that's not me, because I can tell you what I wore to Disneyland when I was four years old: My mother. I thought I was lost. And so, she was checking my etiquette because of course I didn't ask any strangers.

I found officials, I introduced myself kindly, I shook their hand, I told them my problem and asked them to help me solve it. Right. And so, she was taking pictures of me while I thought I was lost at Disneyland. And then she would joke about how much she loved that day. And I said, mother, you do realize that in order for you to have taken photos, you knew where I was the whole time. So, I was never lost. So, you could include me in as a child so that I knew I wasn't lost. And she said, but Mia, it was so delightful to watch you do all of your etiquette to make sure you were okay. And I replied just letting her be her jeez, yes, mom. And she said, and you were okay the whole time and you never cried and you never panicked.

I was scared but I was 4 and even then I knew that would not get me out of trouble, well, it's not my way. It's not my way. I don't tend to cry over silly things. I was raised to be a feminist. I was raised to value myself. I wasn't raised to be man-hating. I was raised right, but I was raised to value me over anything. So, I use it too. I never said this to Richard because he knew because he had a certain way he played games with women and those games didn't work on me. And he was kind of glad because then he knew, Hey, I can trust this one. But then he always had that one eye open, Hey, those others lied two, right. There were three women. He finally told me. Right. I guess it was a year or two and a half or something, two and a quarter where he told me that there were three women who had totally blindsided him, fooled him completely and acted a certain way until they had his trust. And then by the time they blindsided him, you know, he could bear manipulation, and betrayal that just so much, they were just evil waiting to happen. And so, what I always call it is the person they pretended to be didn't exist. It wasn't like they changed over time. Cause in relationships, people evolve and change usually, but some people don't need to evolve and change because they're already the great version of themselves. So, they just get greater; they're not fixing something, but other people know that they're evil.

And they come to destroy you or, you know, be gold diggers or they, have no intention on creating a life or doing anything to make the world better themselves better. They just want, you know, the biggest, most expensive bag to carry, you know, the labels on their shoes, whatever, you know, that kind of stuff.

I was raised to wear classic lines and be dressed well, but to never, you know, be a magnet or a bulletin board for brand names. Like, I don't need you to know that I'm wearing a certain thing. I, you know, like even certain purses I might have, I will take the I won't wear a brand logo. And I take the tags off so that no one knows because I just needed a good, you know, leather quality bag or a fun bag shaped like a popcorn box. You know, that's more, my personality is I was taught quality, classic style (Old Spain and East Coast Classic Lines, and born in California) but I was taught quality as a person and have quality in my ethics. So after a few years, I have boycotted Hawaii because I didn't like the way the native Hawaiians were being treated. And then Richard wanted me to come to Hawaii and I was like, I will only do this for him.

And then I knew someone was hitting us with energy that was astoundingly dark and curses because it was like, we couldn't see each other. He would say things that he couldn't remember. He said, and I didn't know that I was doing the same thing until like a year later when I read through some of the stuff, some of the texts. But the whole time we were there, we were being hit so hard we couldn't function in our normal dance. Every couple has a dance. Some people waltz, some people polka- some people tango and some people dance with the devil. So, I was surprised at the level of hardship and attacks and sadness I had, and he felt for two decades after fighting so hard. Growing up in Richmond, California, ghetto way, he tell me those stories meaning had overcome a lot. And you could tell he was hard and still sweet and such a cutie patootie, but also very when I opened what are people up t.? And he would always joke, as, especially in the early days before the attacks got so great and so targeted Before his phone was stolen and hacking too that. He'd never have to have that one-eyed open mentality or check for motives because I would never be up to anyone.

SPEAK TO WATER

Often when I teach Spirituality Energetic Reality I do the water example CHOOSING CONSCIOUSNESS MAKES GOD CHOOSE TO FLOW THROUGH YOU:

Water must be Solar and must be talked to.

19

TREATING DNA SIGNAL STRENGTH VENICE

When I need to replenish I go to Venice in the 1500s Venice was a world power. It is not an island, it is a Petrified Forest. Remember things we think we see aren't always what they are. I travel the world a lot.

WINTER GOD PROVIDES

...get very weird. So, now she threatened to tell all the secrets she knew, but he still won't say. Then he says, well, I'll just sell part of my company because now I know I can't even be on this same Island because they're casting spells, they're doing attacks, they're affecting his health. So, many things are happening. He now knows he can't even stay on that island because he doesn't want to be close enough for them to do something physically or spiritually. So, he says, I'm going to sell the shares in my company, or I'm going to step down as president and you just send me royalties. They're like, no, you're not going anywhere. So, then they up the negative energy sent some more, make him sick more. So, then he puts his house on sale and says I'll use some money from the sale of the house to leave here, but I'm still going to fight for my worth in this company.

So, that's longer, more black magic, more health problems. The black magic intensifies, they start paying more people. So, not just doing it themselves, not just people, not their family, but actually, start paying people to do it too. Then the house, for some reason it can't sell. No matter when people come, it can't sell. So, then he takes it off the market. Then he goes back. Then they say, see, you're never leaving. You're not leaving because we learn we make more money when you're here. Because even if we take the company, the charm, or whatever that you're flying around doing, we need you to be part of this for us to make more money, so you're stuck. You made this life, you stuck living it. You don't get to go be happy. 18 months pass.

So, then he says, fine. I won't even worry about losing money. I'll take 10 cents on the dollar. I just want out of the company. So, whatever it's worth, I don't know. Maybe you could say a company is worth 10 million. So, you get 1 million when you should've gotten 10 million, but you're willing to take it. So now evil, always a line pusher, a demon is always a line pusher. So, now that they tried to force you to stay because they said you'll only get 10 cents on the dollar. Once you accept that, then they take the deal off the table and say no. No, you can't have 10 cents on the dollar. You get nothing. So, he puts the house back on the market. They do more black magic to block the sale of the house. For some reason, the house will not sell no matter what he does, then the spiritual aspects of the attacks and a blocks He calls and say, oh my goodness, someone's blocking the sale of the house. Don't give up.

Let me find another business to start so maybe that business will make money, make sure that the stuff I put in people's name because I was supposed to be able to love and trust them and I was thinking of taxes or smart business. So, now everything, that's not in my name, that's always mine that I never gave anybody. I only put it in their names. He put it in their names for business reasons. When he goes to get it back now, all those people say, no, we're not giving it back. So, now they won't give back what was never theirs. It's like, They say it's in my name. I'll do what I want. Then he put the house on the market again. Then people started doing stuff to cash like he had written blank checks in case of emergency.

In case of emergency, to him meant I'm not in the country, take this check it's already signed, write the amount you need, and then I'll fix the problem when I get back for the sake of kids, for the sake of business that kind of thing. They start filling out and cashing in the blank checks to break him. People were supposed to come to the house. The buyers were supposed to come the next day he gets home and the dog that's smaller than this, probably this duffle bag size. I've held him so probably about that size poops over 5,000 square feet. Those dogs don't even have enough poop. So, then you know, more black magic.

Now you've been getting diagnoses to see why you're sick, these mystery illnesses and you're starting to get spiritual reasons as the reason because other people who do spiritual stuff are starting to tell you because you're going to them for healing and they're seeing this stuff, but you still don't want to tell me. Now, in Hawaii, there's another man like that, and his wife was doing it, but I met the wife who was bragging about what she was doing to him thinking because I stopped multimillionaire pedophiles as a woman, I would think this is okay to do to your husband. I wondered why I met that woman, Until this started happening. Then a year later, I met another man who had flown in a woman from Eastern Europe. The woman was doing it to him, but I know people he does business with and in my meditations... please hold Oh, we've got a caller.

CINDERELLA WOMEN WHO CAN'T COMPARE WILL BLOCK YOUR MONEY

My parents only taught me The Good things about every race on the planet. Since I was raised with no racism, I saw the world and see the world as energy. I loved every race on the planet. What type of soul are you< not what race are you is what I learned in church, but by using my spiritual gifts, I learned there's more than one type of energetic being. Like Chinese medicine when I finished Chinese medicine School not everything was about the meridians I could see the meridians At school and in my office on a chart, and can see the meridian and watch it move. I could fix them moving blocks and I could see them flowing when they were fixed so I knew Meridians were real. Meridians were science. I did not know people sent energy to hurt meridians.

BEAUTY AND HER BEAST W/O FEAR nor was she given potions by TEMPTATION TO BE FAKE BY ENTICEMENT *OF VERY HANDSOME MEN*

It's not something he would ever have to worry about again, you know, I'd never be up to something I'd never be cheating. I'd never been deceiving. It's not the way that I'm built as a human. And I've proven that on this planet, thousands of times, maybe even 6,000 times, and the choices that I've made in not just what to do, but in what not to do, no matter what hardship energy attacks did had done, done or abroad. There used to be a saying about women. Women are like tea you know, the caliber once she put it in hot water. So, if you had to drink the woman you were with and she was tea, are you drinking? Poison? Are you drinking black tar. Is she camomille? Is she hulong? Is she in empress milk tea? Is she Jasmine? Is she gunmetal? Green? Rose tea? When they're in hot water, that's when you can taste it before they get you into hot water.

So, hopefully, you find someone to love as much as I loved Wei Ming. Now Richard would get on my case for calling him Wei Ming. He would even lie and say like my name's not Wei Ming. And I say, those initials are Wei Ming, you know, your names. And he said, no, I was named after my uncle William. Well, but that was Peter pan. And I was Wendy or sometimes I was 99 and he was Max and I was always Harlequin and he was always the joker and he was so bossy. We would always be Caesar and Cleopatra never Mark Anthony and Cleopatra. And when he was acting all arrogant and ego alpha male, he would be Batman and I would be wonder woman. And when he just had the inner strength and magic, that was his presence, he'd be Superman and I'd be wonder woman because I was wonder woman before I met him.

And he was going between being the tortured soul trying to change like Batman and a good and a warm and perfect heart that lived inside there that was Superman. But Max and 99 were his favorite. I was 99 because I have such a genius mind, and my IQ makes me what's called a 99. And Richard said he was Max because Max adored 99 and valued her and saw her work and was humbled by her skills. So, he had to have her. So, that's what he would say. That's what. It was his favorite Max and 99. And it wasn't in some crazy cosplay way. These were just words for us to say you were acting like, or I love you, like, okay. And I gave up a lot of my life for that promise and they destroyed him for trying to keep it.

You know how I guess the easiest way to explain California would be to have a look at New Orleans. When you look at New Orleans, we see magic everywhere. You see shops. It's part of the tourist advertisement. In California, it's just like Louisiana but when you're a tourist, you may not know there are more shops of magic and there are more types of magic, 72 types of magical communities that we could break in into no more than 40 categories because some of the branches have certain practices within themselves.

THE BEING DIMENSION

No one was judged and everyone was helped.

FALL CLEANS DEBRIS OF ALL SEASONS AND DRIVES THE SEEDS INTO THE GROUND to build our new life.

We live in a very magical world where what we see and seems to be taking place is not magically what's happening at all. I have helped a lot of people see these things over the years. The hidden secrets and motivations, the pain that people are experiencing while we see the smile on their face and the energy that other people are adding to their lives, to give them pain and problems, to keep them trapped, use them, trick them, abuse them while the outside world just sees happy faces.

All Science is Magic Seen and unseen

I was born with a lot of gifts, but clairvoyance means you can see clearly. You can see energy, you can see the world, you can see other worlds. You can see maybe looking at some woman and she seems like she's really pretty, but she's really evil. So, when you look at her, you'll see a beautiful woman and what she wants you to see. When I look at her, I will see an evil creature from a fairy tale. So, she might look like a wolf or she might look like an alligator, or she might look like she has horns. I mean, like in a Snow White kind of horn, not like a stereotypical picture of a devil horn. Because I don't believe necessarily that it looks like that in the spiritual world or the physical world or the real world that kind of thing. I think evil operates more in racism and unkindness and sexism. I worked a lot of years to stop the rape of children. So, I wasn't just saying, please don't rape children. I was healing the victims, but I was also using my other university degrees doing documentaries, TV shows.

We live in a very magical world where what we see and we think is taking place is not magically or energetically what's happening at all. In my life it's always about these things I've been able to see and help people see the energetic things that are happening. Remove patterns.

When I say low vibrational, that's a nonjudgmental way to say dark, mean, evil. I know some people and they view it like this, things that uplift, things that push down or pollute. So, one of my teachers taught me early on that if it doesn't uplift, it's not God meaning sometimes, you know, when you were having a hard time or even if you're having a great time and you get targeted by somebody else's energetic thought like telepathy.

So, those of us who have telepathy will hear not like clairaudience. We don't hear what something is trying to tell us. We hear the stuff people will wish we couldn't find out their secret or not know. We hear God tell us the thought of a being or a soul or of a situation or an object or an animal which is different because a clairaudient would hear if they went somewhere and they're helping an investigative team or they're looking for a lost child. They might hear the things that the child said during their death or during the assault or during the kidnapping or they might hear like in a remote viewing way. They might hear a conversation that the kidnapper is having with the child whereas the clairvoyants will see the child and the kidnapper sitting in the car having this conversation. But they may only see a street sign that they pass that kind of tells them where the car was.

So, where the kid might be alive or dead. But a clairaudient is going to hear the conversation that they're saying. The telepath will hear the thoughts the child is having during that time plus the things the child wants to say, even telling you whether or not they're alive or dead. The telepath will also hear the thoughts of the killer. Are they evil? Are they a demon? Are they human with a childhood that they're telling you or you're seeing their demented brain? It was either a spiritual attack, or it was a spiritual infestation, a spiritual embodiment of some other soul's entity or other soul's energy inside of your body. That would cause mental illness. That's what was believed in the 1800s and there are a lot of Catholic exorcists who believed that that's what all mental illness is now. So, if we take it down a notch in the spiritual world and bring it to the physical world for better understanding. The reason it's called dementia because in the 1800s we believed as a species that all mental illness was a spiritual intrusion.

Betrayals

Richard. He tried to leave Hawaii 17 times, but he was cursed to death. At first Richard was not willing to like, do what we saw all these couples coming together showing the world choose love, right? He was not willing to leave without a fight. He wanted to fight for what he'd earned. He wanted to fight for his ideas. He wanted someone who'd been stealing his money, lying, cheating.

Betraying him in every way possible. He didn't want her to have the money and there was more than one "her", but within the first six months he was like, okay. You know, of course he always says I've been unhappy for 17 years. I'm going to give up, do whatever it takes to be away from this. So, he was willing to take the threat of losing most of his company, losing most of the value of his Percentage of the company.

He just wanted to be out of there and to have a happy life. Now, my business has been taking trauma out of survivors of incest, ritual, abuse, and torture. I've refused a lot of marriage proposals so that I could do my work. And one, in order to protect someone that I loved. So, at that point there had been one proposal I wanted to accept that I hadn't accepted in order to protect them from a vindictive ex.

But this was a proposal that I knew I was going to accept. God had told me months before. No, by that time I was a year before that it was time for me to get married and that I wouldn't have to ever fully retire, but I would have to mostly retire. And that was the message that I had gotten and so, I didn't start looking because you never go around looking. If you go around looking predators will sense that by energetically looking in your space, it's not like intuitive. It is. They will spiritually violate your space, look into it. Just like jealous women that are hollows. They will look into your space when they see you and go stuff like, Oh, a new boyfriend, oh, a new love. And immediately start attacking that so that you don't have your happiness and joy so he didn't tell me any of this. When we first started talking, it was just long talks and long conversations. And. He was much better at slang than I was. I didn't grow up where there was slang and he did. So, he would say he gets to be himself and he gets to be where science and business, you know, that kind of thing. Like for him, there was no part of me that wasn't also like him like accomplished by down to earth. Smart as a whip and hilariously funny. So, it's like nobody, but me gets up at five in the morning for prayer meditation every day, and then runs my house like a 1950s housewife meaning, by four or 5:00 AM, depending on which day, if I wake up early, breakfast is already cooked. Meats are marinating and being flipped for better taste. I know everything in the kitchen. What's for the grocery. There's never dirty laundry. You see, like, it's just constantly a beautiful, happy field, joyful home.

And sometimes when people Are heartless. They think that that is why they were born in order to attack and stop your happiness and joy. There is a metaphysical belief, their spiritual beliefs of. 40 different practices of types of spirituality that believe people do drugs to escape something. So, some drugs people do to escape a past trauma pain.

And other people do drugs to escape the pain of their reality, the pain of where they are. And then there's the books that we all either write, read, study, share that establish amongst the people who do this. If we break them into three parts, then there's one who does it to keep themselves in a lethargic stupor.

Because they can't deal with the environment, they're stuck in so I never judged anyone. It's how I made it. I can't say, I think it always benefits me because I don't think we're supposed to judge people, but sometimes when you don't judge people who don't understand. That I can literally hear their soul will come up and with total really bad intentions, pretending to be a victim.

Well, that works for a little while because I don't tend to or I used to not look into people's space without their permission. Right. And everyone knew that for my NLP mastery for my spiritual gifts. Everyone knew that I will let the universe handle you if you came to fool me, but I'm not going to close my heart to love and not help people who come to me and.

Richard. I thought that was both funny and amazing that somebody can really be just like that good of a person. But he also knew that that partially led me like, you know, Victim to pray. Like, you know, like I don't trust them. Everybody I've ever trusted has done blah, blah, blah, blah, blah. And he was a Scorpio.

So, for him, he like wasn't exactly trusting people anyway. And then where he grew up and I don't believe all the astrological signs. Stereotype to be. That's all of who you are, but normally it is at least part of who you are. Or you wouldn't have been born at that time at that day. At that time, there've been a few weeks cases where people forced births to mess with the numerology or the sign, you know, making someone born too two weeks early or three weeks early changes.

Their birthday and the changes there, Zodiac sign. And then when it's the Chinese years, I always laugh because Richard would always pretend like he's not his year. Like he always liked to pretend they'd be like 59, not 60 because, you know, people that are 60 might not be able to be Peter pan. And it was so funny when I tease him about it, because I was just like, really? So, 58 is young, but 60 is not, you know, that gives you a wrong Chinese year. And he would laugh because I know he, if he plotted out something he wanted, he called it, keeping all the players on the field. So, he was not going to tell me stuff that he would think would make me leave the field.

Right. So, keep the players on the field is what he would say. And what he meant was when he came to see me. In California, one time he brought Jason because Jason had to come right. Then he had to go see his auntie. And then he was like, we'll go to the amusement park in between, right. I'll call you in the morning. And so, he had come. Unannounced. And that was not a problem for me. It was a problem for him because he expected the moment, he called me that I would be there and I would have been, but the moment he called me, my phone was off. Because I was in church, my phone literally was turned off and in my Bag.

So, I had no idea. I don't know if you've ever been to church, but services have singing and services have preaching and there's a lot of Bibles and notes and writing, and I was brought up Baptist and Catholic. So, I used to always say, ``No, that I'm not going to text him, I'm at church, then he'll say, I'm not that much on God. You know, and I'd be like, okay, I understand. Yeah. You know, because for a lot of people if/when continual bad things happen or sometimes people will even force bad things into your life to try to make you lose your faith. So that you think there is no God. So, you may as well let something that God decided should not have a body use your body and exchange for gifts, money, or to be able to like read tarot without spiritual gifts.

Right. Because they're just going to tell you what to tell the people. Well, a lot of people who read. Cards. That's what they do. And then when stuff goes crazy, like the thing they made a deal with starts to take over, they then will call. And say stuff like it's the cards throw away the cards. And I was like, no, it's the thing you made a deal with.

I thought and taught about this for years on my TV show in detail in courses on my radio show. TIME live the now. Let something leave you.

I facilitated my mothers memorial with the Rich Black Lesbians on Martha's Vineyard where her choice will always be honored.

I officiated my father's funeral San Francisco Bay Bridge near the Yacht club to celebrate his love for fishing that bay so he can be in water where he was loved.

Richard's Joss Ceremony burned so long with treasures my cell phone nearly burned up and a thermometer appeared on the screen and my face looked like I had a laser peel. We stood there together for hours then we went home.

As a scuba diver his Hawaiian Ceremony took place off the shore where the dolphin swim.

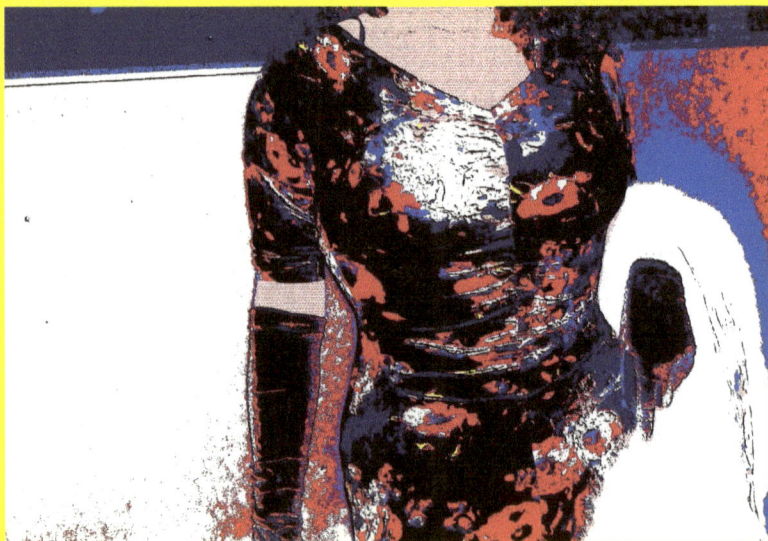

Every moment is the present. Literally and figuratively.

Chapters are exercises

KOI: KING OF INDUSTRY

SPEAK TO WATER

19 TREATING DNA SIGNAL STRENGTH VENICE

WINTER GOD PROVIDES

CINDERELLA WOMEN WHO CAN'T COMPARE WILL BLOCK YOUR MONEY

BEAUTY AND HER BEAST W/O FEAR nor was she given potions by TEMPTATION TO BE FAKE BY ENTICEMENT OF VERY HANDSOME MEN

FALL CLEANS DEBRIS OF ALL SEASONS AND DRIVES THE SEEDS INTO THE GROUND to build our new life.

Betrayals

Every moment is the present. Literally and figuratively.

Mia Morgan White

Sometimes we need to stand up
and be a Hero.

.

www.ingramcontent.com/pod-product-compliance
Lightning Source LLC
Chambersburg PA
CBHW072048090426

42733CB00033B/2473